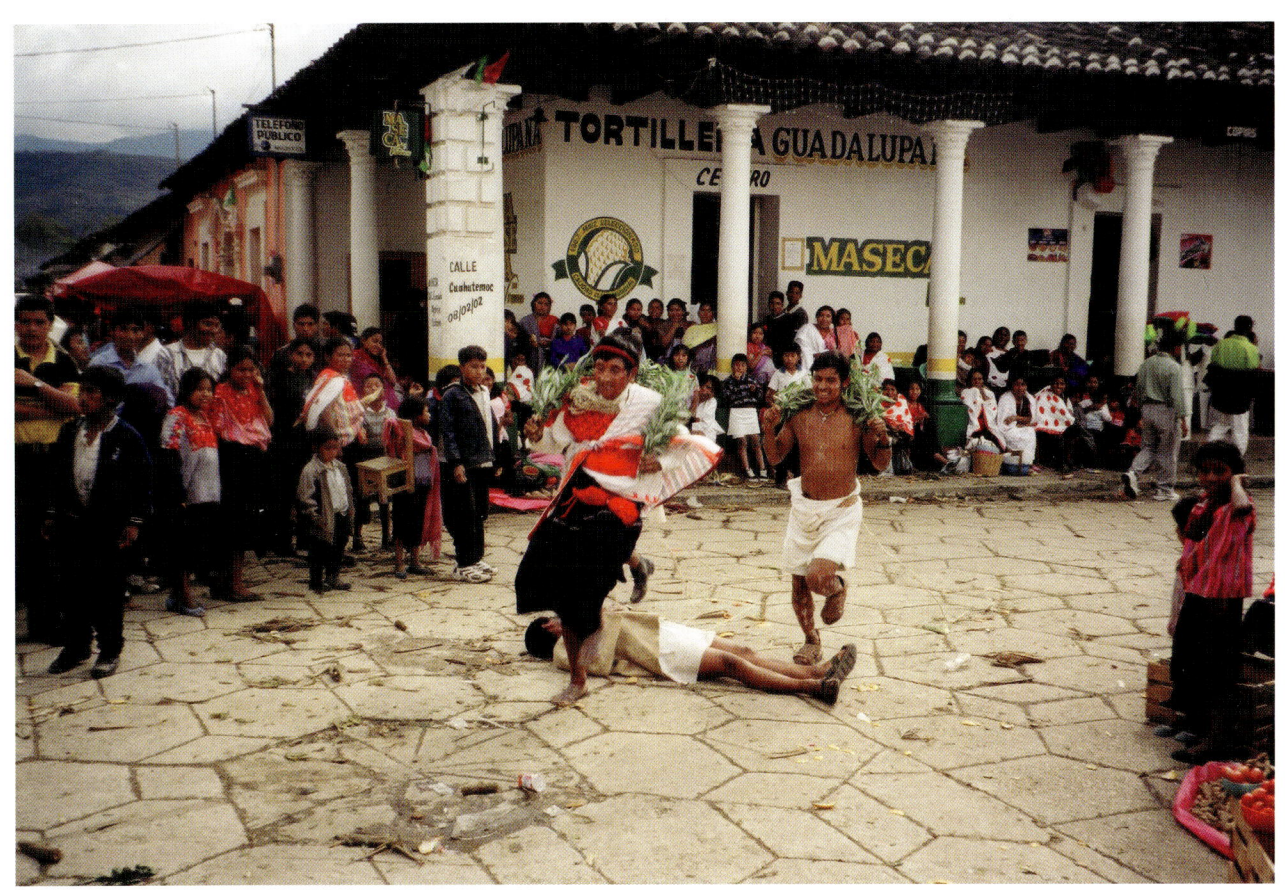

"In the município of Chilón the old
people say, 'If there weren't men
in skirts, it wasn't a fiesta.'"
                    Padre Eugenio Maurer

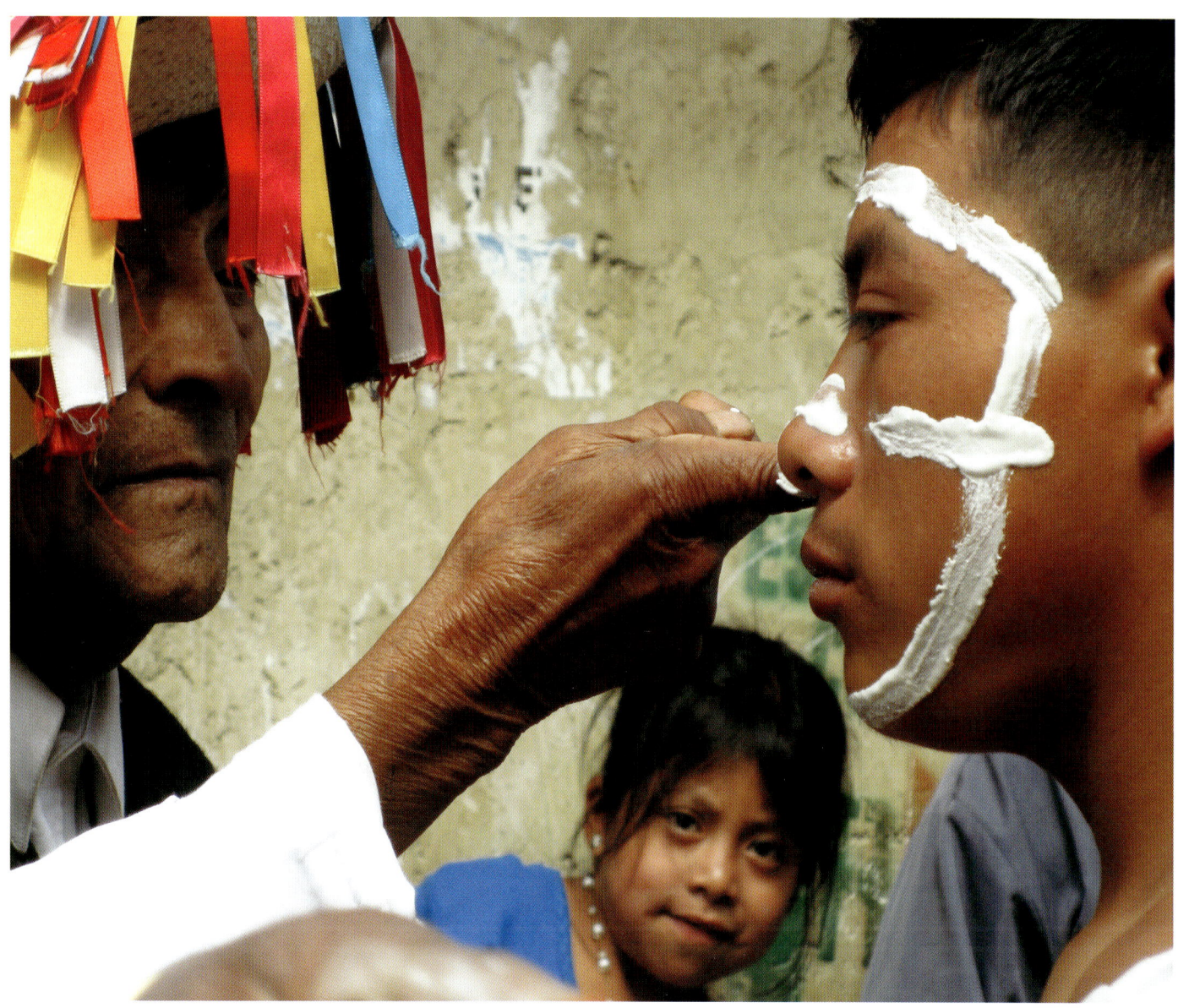

Men In Skirts

The fiesta of Nazarena or Tajimoltik in Chenalho', Chiapas

Carter Wilson

photographs by Ámbar Past and Carter Wilson

bankilal books

First Edition 2025

ISBN 978-0-938531-08-1
1. Chiapas (Mexico) 2. Cultural Anthropology 3. Highland Maya fiestas
4. Male cross-dressing performers 5. Holy clowns

Design & Layout
Macduff Everton

Typeface used in this book is Adobe Jenson Pro/ Adobe Jenson is an old-style serif
typeface drawn for Adobe Systems by its chief type designer Robert Slimbach. Its
Roman styles are based on a text face cut by Nicolas Jenson in Venice around 1470,
and its italics are based on those created by Ludovico Vicentino degli Arrighi fifty
years later. It's an organic design, with a low x-height. It is considered a highly readable
typeface and is accordingly often used in book design for body text.

Printed in South Korea on acid-free paper.

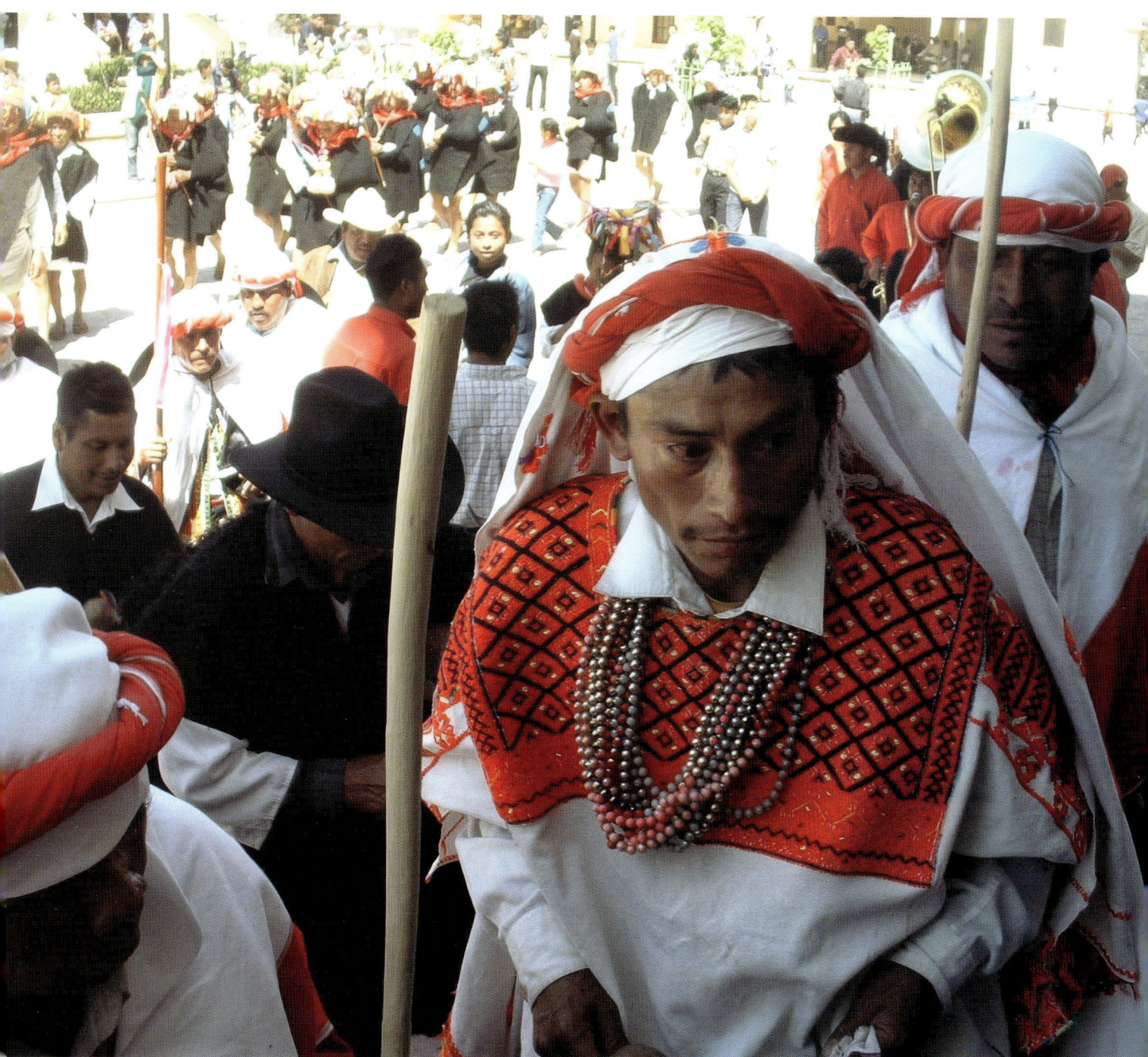

The Abductress emters church.

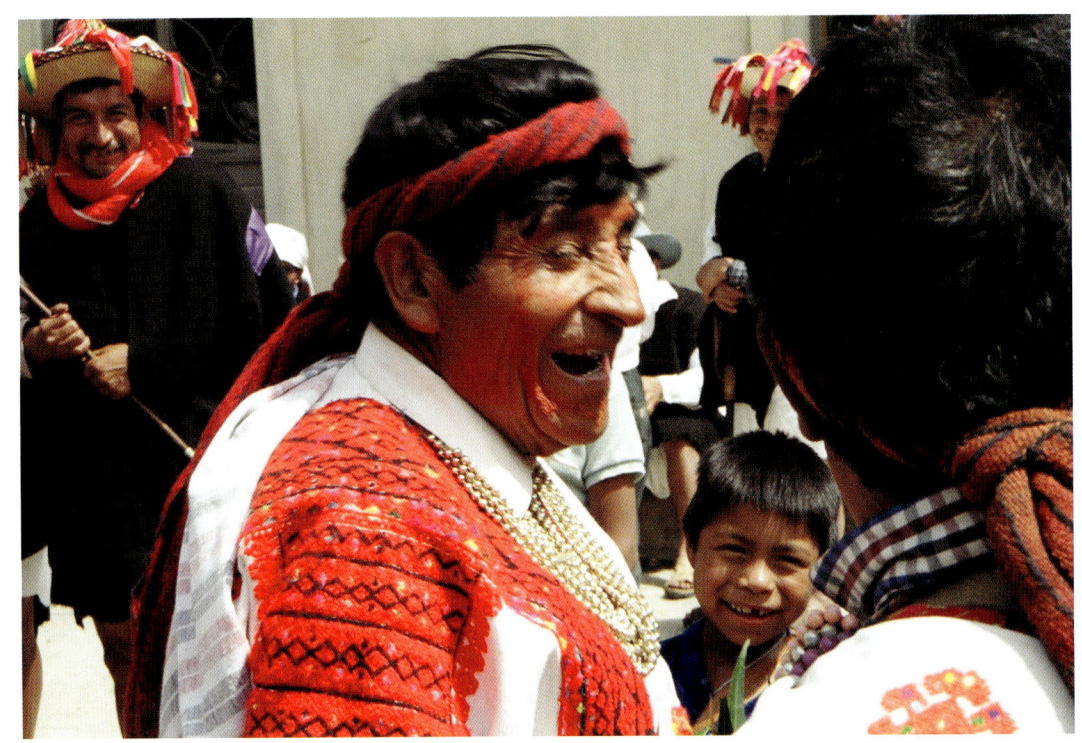

If you don't have humor along with the rest, you can't access the supernatural. What spirits want to come around mopey whiney solemn beings?

Leslie Marmon Silko

Preface

In *The Zuni Man-Woman*, author Will Roscoe recounts the life of We'wha, a 19th century Zuni who was biologically male and culturally female. One of Roscoe's concerns is how information about sexuality and gender roles in other societies can be used against a vulnerable people. I share this worry. In the case of Zuni, the unguarded accounts of ceremonial life by the first generation of white anthropologists were employed viciously by others to portray indigenous people as lewd, ungodly savages and thus to give white settlers reason to seize land and other resources from the pueblo. Roscoe's cautionary tale from the past is a reminder that cultural relativism, a liberal idea, is in no way universally accepted, and continues to bear heavy practical political implications for minority people.

Toward the end of this book, I describe an event which is called sometimes "The Ceremony of the Mat." It takes place eight times with two sets of actors in the late afternoon of the Monday of a Maya fiesta in the mountains of southern Mexico. Staged in the homes of religious officials, the little drama involves a mythic lady, the *Me'kabinal* or Jungle Mother played by a man and her helpers, the *Kuruspatetik* or Crossbacks, two nearly naked fellows with crosses on their chests and backs and red and white jaguar spots painted over much of the rest of their bodies. All three have masks outlined on their faces, the Mother's red and the Crossbacks' white. The trio get down and pretend to sleep hidden under a straw mat on the dirt floor. Three *Ik'aletik* or Blackmen, powerful, comic "evil" spirits, come looking for them, claiming the Jungle Mother is their "aunt." When they discover the three, they lift their legs and simulate having sex with them. Once they are finished, the Blackmen fall down in post-coital exhaustion and themselves pretend to sleep. The lady and her assistants awake and in retribution fake sex with the Blackmen. As part of the speechifying, all loaded with heavy sexual inuendo, children are encouraged to pay attention to the proceedings so they will learn how to make babies and—importantly—understand how sex should be a reciprocal matter, giving pleasure to both parties.

The large crowd squeezed into the official's house laugh loudly at all of this, children sometimes a little shyly. The Blackmen and the mythic lady elaborate, adding in new lewd jokes, including on occasion references to current Mexican politics or gringos like me and my friend Ámbar Past with our ubiquitous cameras and tape recorders. The entire audience knows the play is a farce, the actors honorable people in real life, their performances well-regarded community service. As a form of sex education for the young, the play is both raucous and raw and yet subtle and sublime at the same time.

This is a book primarily about the performance of the Jungle Mother and her two assistants on the Monday of an annual fiesta called *Tajimoltik*, the Festival of Games, in the town of Chenalhó. (The fiesta is also called *Nazarena* or The Nazarene, and the Jungle Mother and the Crossbacks also represent Jesus Christ in their body paint.) But this "Mother" is not the only man in skirts who shows up on busy Monday, there are three other major transvestites as well—the *Me'el* or Mother of Mothers, the *Sak'il* or Abductress, and the Guatemalan Woman, as well as a large volunteer contingent of men and boys called the *Antsilal J'ak'otetik*, Dancing Women. While other events are also in progress, Monday of the Festival of Games is markedly a virtual explosion of men in drag.

In the United States at the present moment my own society has entered on a protracted period of struggle between factions regarding sex and gender roles. A large number of states are busy enacting legislation not only to take away from women control of their own bodies, but also to get sex education out of all k-12 schooling. Conservatives would prefer to keep knowledge of the existence of alternate sexualities (i.e., homosexuality) away from young people entirely. Much of the legislation is about thwarting transsexuals' gender choices, which comes down to punishing them for being who they feel they are. As a result, I offer this material with some trepidation, and in the hope that it won't be used to denigrate the people of Chenalhó, who have been exceedingly kind to me.

Cultural anthropologists who write about fiestas usually try to explain everything that occurs in the set rituals of such occasions. I make no such claim to completeness or full explication. For eight or so years in the early 2000s I attended the Festival of Games in Chenalhó in Chiapas, always with my friend Ámbar Past. She had long associations with people in the town and her Mayan Tsotsil is excellent. (My own, gotten 60 years ago, was never more than serviceable and now is hardly even that.) Ámbar and I came along as spectators and for fun, not as serious ethnographers. In the process we fell in with the group called the *Jtoyk'in* or Fiesta Raisers. Though the characters they represent are figures from history and mythology and their performances are advertised as scary or dangerous, no one is fooled. These are comic characters, holy clowns.

With permission over the years we took a lot of photographs and were allowed to tape record speeches. We asked questions when it seemed appropriate and visited some of the Fiesta Raisers at their homes in the countryside. We profited greatly from previous written descriptions of the fiesta, especially the work of Calixta Guiteras-Holmes from the 1940s and 50s and Victoria Reifler Bricker in the 1960s and 70s, but also from the more recent insights of Christine Eber and Walter F. "Chip" Morris. Scholar and writer Jacinto Arias Pérez, a *Chenalero* or *Pedrano* himself, provided insight and a key text (tales of the god-man *Ojoroshtotil*) for which I am very grateful. But even with all this help, my understanding of the Monday events remains limited.

Anthropologist and cybernetic thinker Gregory Bateson advised marking the point where your thinking on a problem has run its course. Leave a stone in the path or tie a handkerchief around a tree so others will know how far you have come. Now that I am over 80 and my walking is not good, it is unlikely I will be able to go back to the Festival of Games again, so it is here I have to tie my Batesonian handkerchief or set my Gregorian stone to indicate how far I have come, firm in the admission of my limits, and in the hope that my personal memories and the photographic record will provide at least a taste of one wild Monday in Chiapas.

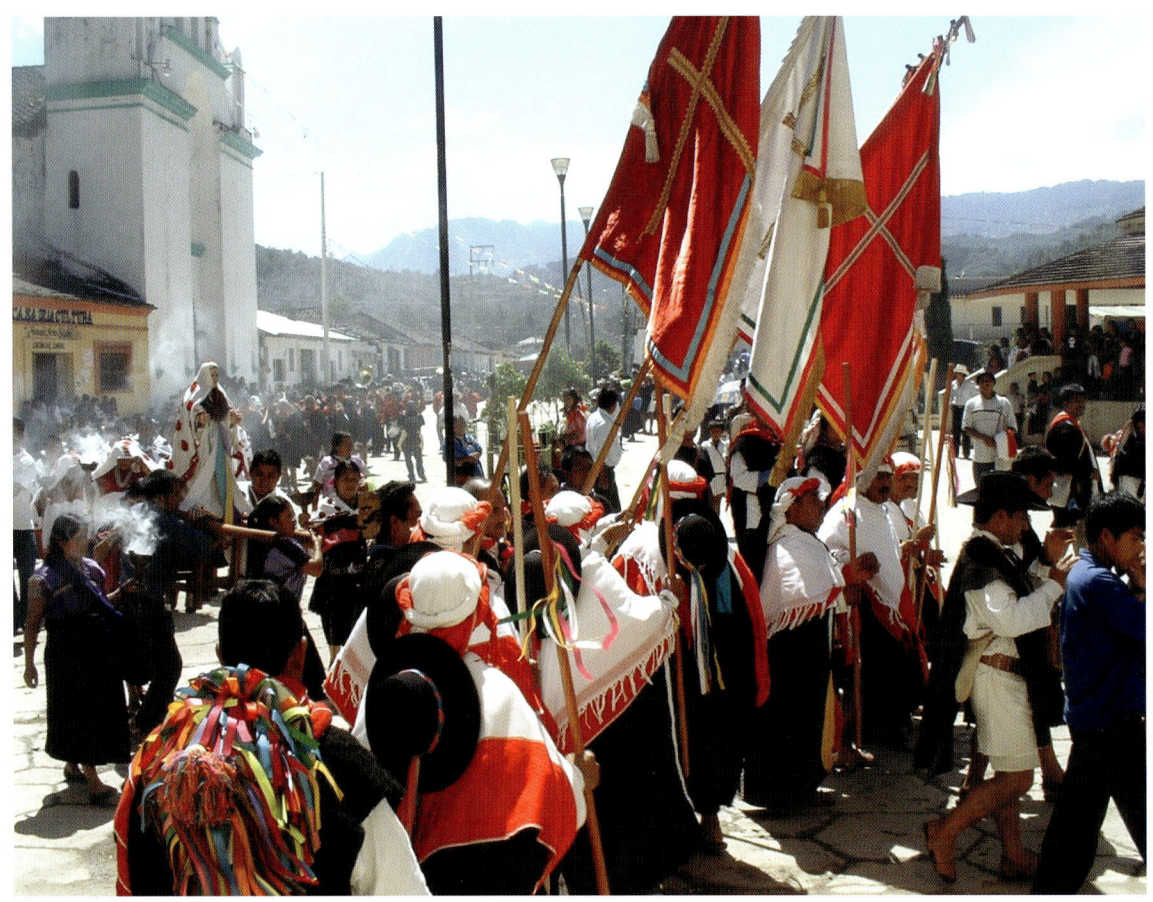

Fiesta in Chenalho'

June 23, 1963: The day the hook was set

In my last semester of college Professor Evon Z. Vogt at Harvard's Department of Social Relations gave me a Carnegie Foundation grant for a summer of field work in southern Mexico. "Vogtie," as everyone called him, was then six years into a large collective study of Zinacantán, a Maya Tsotsil municipio in the Chiapas highlands. I don't know exactly why he chose me. True I had Spanish in high school and the previous summer a school friend and I had driven from Washington, DC to Mexico City to have a look around. But I was an English history and literature undergraduate major and had interests but only two college courses in the social sciences. Sometimes I thought the real reason Vogtie took me on may have been my height (I am 6'5"). The two previous summers he'd managed to place a student named Eric Prokosch in the more closed municipio adjacent to Zinacantán called Chamula, so maybe he slated me mainly so the big guy could keep that door open.

That summer Vogtie was busy with some other business and did not arrive in Chiapas until August. We, six Carnegie students and a graduate student named Victoria Reifler, who was there to learn Tsotsil in advance of her dissertation field work, were supervised by a man named George Collier. George had been my college classmate, but he graduated a year ahead of me and was married to a brilliant Radcliffe student named Jane Fishburne. George and Jane already had several summers of Chiapas field work and a year as graduate students completed. Their first child was born in Mexico City toward the end of June, 1963, just as we Carnegie students were arriving.

On a Saturday our little group reached San Cristóbal de Las Casas, the ladino (or "white" or "Spanish-speaking") city that serves as the commercial and governmental hub for the numerous indigenous communities around it. Sunday morning George came by our frigid, bare-bones hotel in his VW van and took us out to Chamula to see the Sunday market and the "mero dia" or big day of the fiesta of San Juan Bautista, Chamula's patron saint. (This was June 23; on the Catholic calendar the saint's day is the 24th.)

I had respect and fondness for George. A discreet, gentle, even diffident, civil sort of man. While now at least technically my boss, he found a comradely tone to take with me which preserved our sense of also being classmates and, in that at least, equals.

Chamula's town center lay in the heart of a large valley. There was a gigantic plaza, a huge imposing white church, a one-story municipal building, a school and a medical clinic, a little row of shops. The hillsides all around were dotted with traditional mud-wall, steep-roofed thatch houses. As soon as we got down from the van my fears about what I had gotten myself into rose up as a lump in my throat (globus hystericus in medical parlance). The plaza was filled with vendors at little stands or sitting on the ground by small stacks of vegetables, fruit, or pottery or other goods displayed on tarps, all in the midst of a huge flowing mass of men, women, and children in wool outfits, belted white chamarras or tunics and cowboy hats for the men, full-length black skirts, shawls, and ribbon-braided hair for the women. It felt as though everyone was staring at us or laughing behind their hands, making comments we of course could not understand. Suddenly turned into zoo animals, our little contingent clung together, trying bravely to smile, be no threat. Corn husks and other detritus underfoot, a long row of men and boys with their tunics pulled to the side pissing against a fence down from the plaza, a rich shit smell competing with the smell of burning charcoal, gunpowder, and (though I couldn't identify it yet) sweet piney copal incense. Over the three principal days of San Juan ten thousand people might come in to town from the surrounding hamlets, George said. Though there were a couple of outhouses behind the cabildo or government building, most people would defecate outdoors. Noise. Church bells and a loud brass oompah band, skyrockets whooshing up into the blue and exploding with a puff of white smoke and then a bang. Spent ones clattering to the ground dangerously near you. Busy groups of officials in black with broad ribboned hats and silver-headed canes hurrying to and fro on some kind of business, the way before them cleared by squadrons of pushy young men with black staves slung over their shoulders. The town police or *Mayoletik*, according to George. Women carrying smoldering pots of incense scurried along behind some of the men's groups. Tingly harps and guitars, scrappy violins, drums, shrill flutes.

More calm in the dark interior of the enormous church, a place of echoes, long shafts of blue light from windows high on the walls, whole families on their knees before rows of candles laid out in front of 20 or so white-faced saints standing along the walls, small mirrors hung on ribbons on their chests, a carpet of pine needles spread across the floor, people praying in a kind of repetitive singing or chanting, others chatting, saluting each other with little glasses of clear homemade rum, men lighting cigarettes off each other. When babies in shawls on their mothers' backs cried fretfully the mothers swung them around and gave them a nipple to suck.

It was just high noon—the church bells clanging insistently, many rockets going up--BOOM! BOOM! BOOM!—when we got ready to leave, but there were already people passed out or wandering around drunk, mostly men, but women too, weeping, singing. On the road up out of the valley, George told me in Zinacantán he usually avoided the fiestas—confusing, too much going on at once and hard to make sense of.

George had the knowledge and the experience. Yet even in the moment I was aware I didn't agree. And so June 23, 1963 became the day my fascination with the intricacies and the mysteries and the great pleasures of Maya fiestas began.

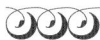

My little brother, only 78 now, says he does not remember a moment in our childhood when I was not putting on a show of some sort or another. Popsicle stick puppets of Goldilocks and the Three Bears in a shoebox theater, parades around the block of all the neighbor kids I could corral into donning their Halloween costumes and festooning their tricycles or scooters with crepe paper streamers after I'd seen the "walk arounds" at the Ringlng Brothers Circus. Then marionettes and me as a bear in a third-grade "Hansel and Gretel," later a home sci-fi drama with me as a space traveler landing and encountering my brother, who played The Martian. And of course a part in every school play thereafter, up through high school. Directing the kids' water ballet for Parents Day at a summer camp. In college I mostly wrote the shows, though I occasionally directed and once warbled half of a Frank Loesser duet in my unreliable baritone.

No wonder I was attracted to highland Maya fiestas, a form of communal theater with a long-used script or series of stipulated events participated in by a large number of people, many of whom flow back and forth between being actors and members of the attentive audience.

That first summer I lived in the family of a Chamula Escrivano or scribe. Mariano's job required him to be at the cabildo in the town center most days. I went with him. He took it as his responsibility to watch out for me and explain the oddity of my being there to others when he had to. Mariano's more regular work was teaching civil officials, men usually corn farmers but currently occupying one-year positions in civil government, in how to perform the rituals required of them. Thus it was that within six weeks of coming to Chamula

I could be found passed out at the home of an official called a *Kominarol* or Governor sleeping on the floor drawn up around the embers of the fire in the center of the room with the Governor's grown boys and Mariano under blankets the *Me'Kominarol* or Governor Wife had spread over us. We had spent the evening scrubbing the Governor's silver-headed cane of office with salt in a big gourd bowl of homemade rum, or *pox* [Tsotsil 'x' sounds like English 'sh'], which custom dictated we had to consume down to the last drop once the washing was done. And why that? Because the Governor, his family, and Mariano and his were all due at seven the following morning in Zinacantán, a ten or so kilometer walk away through the mountains, in order to represent Chamula in honoring their patron, San Lorenzo (Saint Lawrence), on the big day of his fiesta. Rousing ourselves, about 3 a.m. we set out in bright moonlight for Mariano's house 45 minutes down the road, added his wife and five children to our group and then proceeded on, carrying the sleeping little ones, to the difficult slippery path that descended into the valley of Zinacantán. There we met up with the rest of Chamula civil officialdom, went to pray in the Zinacantecos' beautiful white church and then sat on a stone shelf along the outer wall of the churchyard where bottles appeared from net bags and we all drank again, wives and daughters settled on the ground before us on their folded rebozos, also toasting each other and drinking.

I was 21 and had some stamina.

The next winter with more work in Chiapas I made a point of getting there in time for the Chamula Festival of Games, or Carnival, an arduous, long fiesta which features among other things a nighttime "war" where men on both sides of the battle line fling horse turds at one another. On Tuesday afternoon men dressed up as a cross between monkeys and 19th century French soldiers carrying flags gallop mostly barefoot back and forth across a grid of old roof thatch laid on the ground and set aflame. By now, I was a more common sight in town. One night when the officials were praying in the church, the man accompanying them playing the *Bolom Chon* or Jaguar Song on a homemade guitar asked would I fill in for him for a while. I puffed with pride. (The Bolom Chon has only two chords, so I was able to get along through it.)

In 1964 there was not a lot we students could read about the highland indigenous communities, and we often did not know how to connect what we were seeing with what did exist in the historical and archeological record. That spring I was surprised and pleased to learn people still used the old Maya calendar with the 18 months of 20 days each and the five-day evil or at least wild and dangerous "lost month" or *Chay K'in*, which falls around the time of Catholic Carnival (or Mardi Gras) in February. Today it has become a commonplace to call the unique fiestas celebrated in this period ceremonies of "year renewal," a term from Diego de Landa, the 16th century Spanish bishop who first described Maya life in the Yucatán.

In 1964 I worked in a group study of drinking in several highland towns sponsored by the National Institute of Mental Health. Rather than participant/observation we interviewed community members in their own languages. Since I knew only a little Tsotsil, I was coupled with one of the principal investigators, anthropological linguist Gerald Williams. Gerry did not know Tsotsil either, but he knew how to get into it, sketch the grammar, figure out the phonemes, so while we were collecting "data" I was also learning the rudiments of speaking. Xun Okotz and Xun Méndes Tsotsek, the Chamula men we worked with most closely, had clear, precise knowledge about how drinking takes place on a variety of occasions—at baptisms, funerals, fiestas. It did not occur to me at first, but later I understood their particular knowledge about fiestas came not from having served the official religious positions themselves, but from being among the large number of volunteer assistants called on to help office-holders with what is called a *cargo* in Spanish or one's *abtel* or "work" in Tsotsil.

Two years later I was back again with the anthropologist Duane Metzger and filmmakers Arnold Baskin and Michael Swigert to make a documentary about the fiesta of Santiago (Saint James), the namesake saint of Tenejapa, a Tseltal-language município that borders Chamula to the west. One of the first things Metzger did was to hire four prestigious local men to work on the film with us. In the sleepy quiet of the weeks prior to the big days, I could not understand quite why he had done this. But once the town filled up with people and we began to trail along after two of the major religious players, I realized these four gentlemen were subtly and pleasantly quelling people's suspicions of our cameras and tape recorders, letting them know we had been approved by the town government. The result of the effort was a 28-minute film called "Appeals to Santiago," still available on Youtube: https://www.youtube.com/watch?v=HKG94SRJtg4

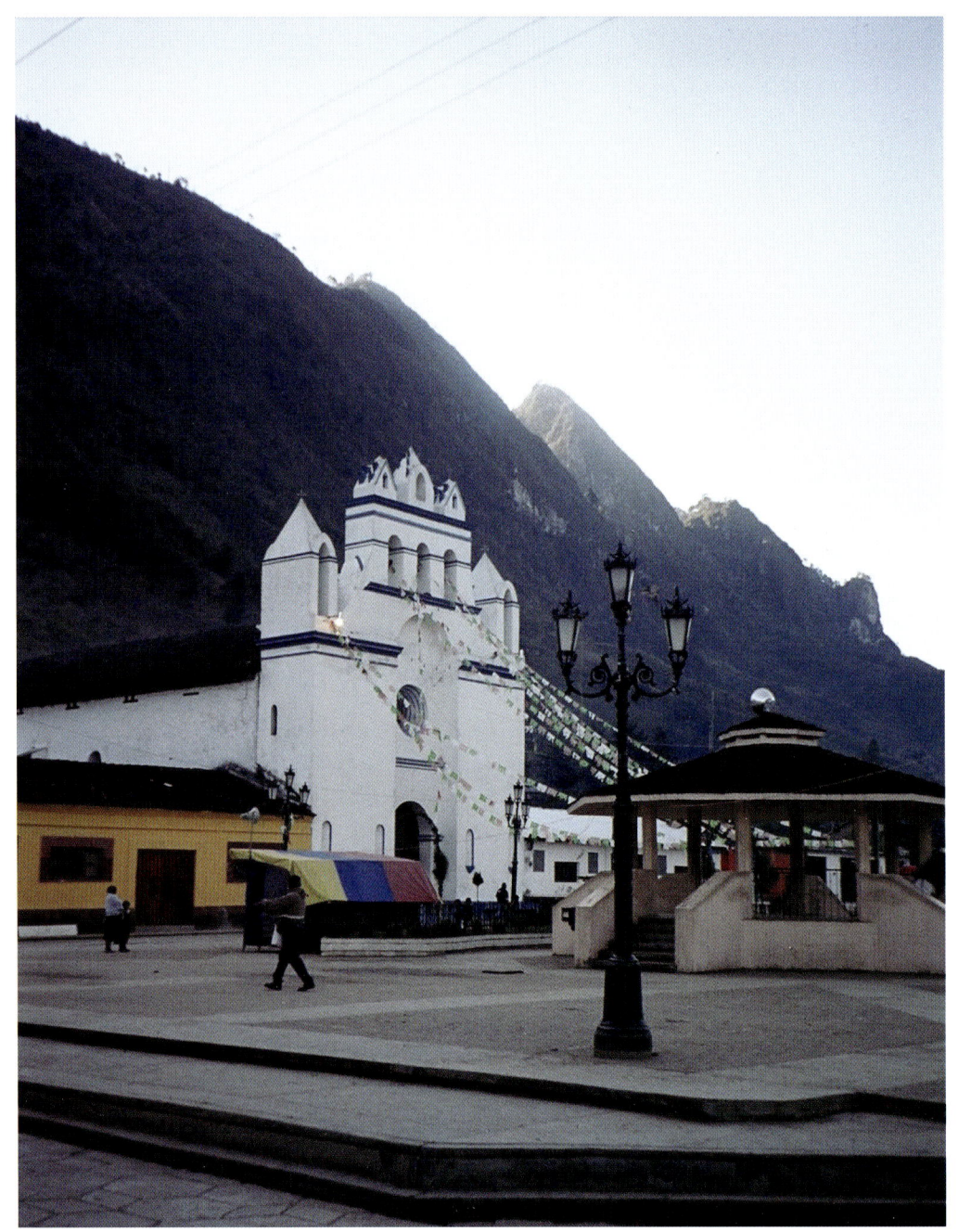

Church in Chenalho'

In the old days (for me the 1960s) from San Cristóbal to the closer-in indigenous towns you paid a peso for passage on a truck. They nosed in along the curbs on the street by the old market, the driver's assistant, the *ayudante*, put out a wooden ladder four or so feet long and helped women, little children, men with big bultos or sacks of corn, and the occasional gringo get up and in. Sometimes there were benches along the railings where women and children could sit, but men mostly rode standing up, shoulder to shoulder and swaying along, sometimes grabbing the siding or each other to stay vertical as we tilted along the deep-rutted roads. If it began to rain seriously, the driver would pull off and the ayudante would throw a tarp over the ridge pole and lash it down outside at the corners.

Today there are taxis and *combis* (VW buses) and the departure points for the different towns are in various parts of the extensive new market on the far side of town. The combis often have an extra seat put in so they can carry 14 or so people, and the *taxistas* won't set out until their cars have five, maybe six, passengers. If you're impatient, you can pay extra and the driver will start without a full load. My friends Ámbar Past and Andrew Mutter and I were in no hurry, though, so we waited in the back seat of the cab in a dark shed, Andrew with his little white and spotted terrier Gringo on his lap, sniffing expectantly at the half-open window. The dog had been everywhere with Andrew, himself a slender, well-educated Brit. Even in a new city, he said, Gringo set his own itinerary, disappearing when he cared to, roaming about even complex crowded metropolises like Rome but always coming back to Andrew by nightfall. Should Andrew change lodging during the day, his sidekick seemed to know where to find him. A polite, reserved fellow traveler.

The roads up into the Tsotsil-speaking municípios are paved now, but still they wind in large arcs as we climb through the winter bald hills of Chamula to a nearly 7,000 foot high ridge and then cross into the município of Chenalho' and start down a long sweeping back and forth glide to the town itself. The taxistas are almost all boys or young men with bald tires and no driver's licenses and they take chances, shifting out of gear or even turning off their engines on the downhills to save gas. Best not to concentrate on the dangers of this form of travel.

The center of Chenalho' is close to the south end of the township. The rest of the município then slopes down toward hotter country to the north, where in addition to corn they can grow coffee as a cash crop. Along the road past the town center are the settlements of Polho', Los Chorros, and Acteal, where in 1997 45 supporters of the Zapatistas were murdered by men believed to be agents of the Mexican government.

The taxista leaves us in the nearly empty plaza before the imposing façade of the church. Across from it a big stand of painted blue wooden crosses. The fiesta of Tajimoltik is in progress, but Sunday's events are over, many houses are closed up, wood smoke from the evening cooking fires seeps out from under the eaves of the tile roofs. The sun has set beyond the town's steep sidewalls and dusk and chill are coming on.

We truck along down one street a couple blocks, Andrew with his sleeping bag and Ámbar and I with cotton blankets under our arms, Ámbar also lugging a large plastic bag of groceries. At the door of what she thinks is the home of her friends Benancio and Verónica we knock. Dogs inside bark furiously. Andrew's terrier sniffs at the bottom of the door, but for nearly a minute no one comes. Then yes, she was right, a man with a mustache in a white tunic opens up. Right behind him a little woman peers up over his shoulder. A small child clings to her skirt. Big hellos for Ámbar, a hug from the woman, soft handshakes and smiles for Andrew and me from Benancio. Ámbar asks can we stay with them for the fiesta and they say of course and usher us inside.

The house's front room is devoted to storage, bags of dried corn and maybe some of coffee beans against the walls. Behind it, the room with Verónica's cooking fire in the center of the floor where we will lay out our bedding tonight. Beyond that a little courtyard and another room we can't see into where the family sleeps. Children come in somewhat shyly to be introduced. Mikel, Lucia, a baby in the shawl on Verónica's back, older boys, one of whose voice has deepened. The oldest girl has her own baby, one that she has adopted. Ámbar offers Veronica things from the San Cristóbal market, a cut-up chicken in a plastic bag, onions, carrots, zucchini, which Verónica accepts with laughter and obvious pleasure. All of it will appear later on in a soup we will share.

I bring Benancio greetings from Marcey Jacobson, a photographer who has lived almost 50 years in San Cristóbal, and who is one of his godmothers (in Tsotsil his *ch'ulme'* or sacred mother). Marcey and her partner Janet Marren were friends of Benancio's father, a storied figure in Chenalho' called Mol ("Old") Komate, who was the town's *Maestro Sonobil* or Music Master and also advisor to officials about how to perform in Carnival, a post Benancio has inherited. Ámbar knew Mol Komate and his wife, so the goodwill card we called on when we asked for *posada* (lodging) is an old established one.

We go out to take a walk around. A river runs alongside the edge of town, and in the stillness of evening you hear its constant churn. Though I have never been here before, I lived the summer we were making our film about 25 miles away in Tenejapa, where the "center" has the same mix of indigenous people and ladinos as Chenalho'. White plastered adobe houses line eight or a dozen or so paved or half-paved streets. Some have the front room turned into a little store with a low wooden gate to keep dogs and small children out. In some of the tiendas the single bulb on a cord hanging down over the merchandise has already been turned on. Light and ranchero music come from a bar restaurant on the far side of the plaza, the major hangout of the ladinos. The town's only pay phone is in there.

We run into a big-bellied smiley gentleman with gold caps on most of his front teeth. Crinkly lines around his eyes, light mahogany skin, white cotton shorts and shirt. Out for a walk himself or a look around, he says. Ámbar knows him from years of coming to this fiesta. He's one of the principal transvestites in the Festival of Games, called the Me'el or "Mother of Mothers" as Ámbar translates it. At first he doesn't seem to recognize her and then promptly he does. He is jolly and expansive, all laughter and jokes with us. Well, at least with Ámbar. I confuse him some because of how little Tsotsil I remember. It takes him a while to realize he needs to treat me like a little child with small simple sentences, or at least to add some Spanish to the mix in the talk. But no problem, he adjusts. He is 60, he tells us. He served as the Mother of Mothers for 20 years and then stepped down. The whole Fiesta Raisers group retired. But the men who replaced them didn't prove up to the job and now the old gang is back at it. He invites us to come visit him sometime in Los Chorros where he lives. Down there we're all PRI (Partido Revolucionario Institucionál), he assures us.

To me a reminder of the turmoil Chenalho' has endured in recent years, divisions that opened up when people became adherents of different religious and political movements, joining *catechista* (catechist or Catholic revival) groups, some declaring themselves supporters of the Zapatista rebels down in the Lacandón jungle. A "peace-keeping" occupation by the Mexican army, removal of Chenalho's longtime Catholic priest Padre Miguel Chanteau as a potential troublemaker, then the awful murder of people driven from their homes camped out and defenseless down at Acteal. By noting that he supports PRI, the Mother is telling us that corrupt as it may have become he is an adherent of the old political stability which PRI provided Mexico for over 60 years.

Back at Benancio and Verónica's by dark, reminiscing begins. Laughter over how the gringas Marcey and Janet originally had not understood how rigorous the responsibilities of becoming godparents in Chenalho' might be, Mol Komate arriving in San Cristóbal to inform them their godchild Benancio needed school books, then needed a flute, then a drum, finally a bicycle. Benancio grinning, amused, but mostly silent when attention focuses on him, the older children in and out of the room, watching or half-watching a Mexican movie on the small television in the corner. I think Veronica says she is 45, which would make her seven or eight years older than her husband. She and Ámbar talk while she cooks on her knees at her big round *comal* or griddle.

Ámbar's Tsotsil is so good she can joke freely in it. She tells a story about Mol Komate from almost thirty years ago. She was traveling through several of the munícipios with Antonio Turok while he photographed, Mol Komate along as their guide. In Chamula they came upon a pond or a little lake and it being still the hippy period the young people promptly shed their clothes and went swimming. Local residents showed up and expressed outrage to Mol Komate who, according to Ámbar, told them, "Don't you know anything? You're just hicks! In Chiapa de Corzo or Mexico City nowadays men and women both just take off their clothes and go around nude at the drop of a hat," which apparently mollified the local people.

We are served coffee, then bowls of delicious, cooked baby turnips with their greens, and then Verónica prepares omelets for us. For each one she cracks two eggs onto her comal, then salts them, stirs them with her finger, and, when they are done, plucks them up and serves them wrapped in a tortilla.

They have two small cats, one gray-and-calico, the other orange-white. The gray one has a string around her neck and an old, beat-up huarache tied to it. Why is this? Well, apparently it's punishment for the cat having grabbed off some meat being smoked over the fire. The cat seems not to mind, however. She drags her sandal around after her and then climbs on it to sit or lie down and sleep so close to the embers of the fire her coat becomes a little singed on one side.

At some point I manage to say to Verónica in Tsotsil, "You have a lot of cats."

She is pensive, considering. Then says, straight-faced, "Yes, so many when we run out of firewood we just use cats instead."

Even the nodding smaller children know she's kidding.

Benancio needs to go to bed, has to be up at 2 a.m., he says. Verónica gets out plastic sacks for us to lay on the floor and brings additional cotton blankets for us. We are told to come through to the back patio if we need to, there is a toilet there.

(Later I tried the bathroom. In a shed so low I couldn't stand up fully was a built-up slab and below a large PVC pipe with a half-section cut out of it. You squatted and aimed and hoped to get in the hole. Then a spigot nearby and you ran water until the poop and the toilet paper began to move along down the pipe, apparently into the town sewage system.)

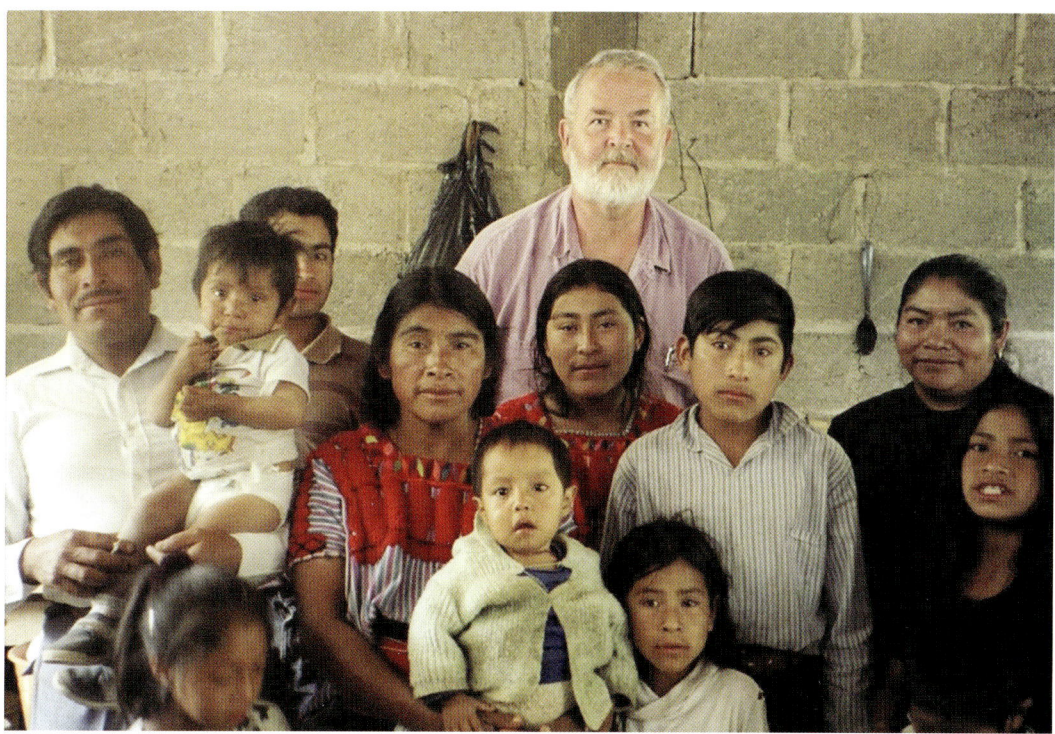

Benancio and Verónica's family, el gringo, and 2nd in from right Petra Ernandes, a friend from Chamula

When are you leaving? When are you coming back?

Gary Bevington's *Maya for Travelers and Students* is a guide to learning the indigenous language of Yucatán and also an entirely useful primer for how to get a new language on your own. But it is more than that. Bevington, himself a linguist, plunked down in a Mayan-speaking town on the peninsula and in addition to language-learning technique he offers great advice about how to integrate yourself into another culture.

At the outset he predicts that soon after you arrive in a Yucatec village the people will ask you, "When are you leaving?" But don't be put off, he says, for soon they will ask, "When are you coming back?"

Those of us who have had the good fortune to live for a time in indigenous Maya communities may not always realize the special quality of the hospitality. Certainly outsiders can be greeted with fear and suspicion that they might be witches or evil spirits, or unknowingly harbor such in themselves. In periods of conflict, the highland towns have been less friendly. The anthropologist Ruth Bunzel was forced out of Chamula in 1940, and Calixta Guitieras-Holmes had to quit the Tseltal municipio of Oxchuc when Oxchuc was divided by warring factions of protestant converts and followers of the older "Maya-Catholic" religion. Subsequently Guitieras-Holmes found a more tolerant environment which led to her ethnography of Chenalho' *Perils of the Soul.*

But openness to interested strangers remains more likely, as Bevington points out. In the eight years that Ámbar and I attended the Festival of Games, I noticed the members the Fiesta Raisers more and more amused to see us when we showed up.

The reason? Nowadays among Maya-speaking people of southern Mexico and Guatemala there is a new version of consciousness of their own value. There was an older version too. Outcast, brutally exploited ever since the Spanish invasion over 500 years ago, and despite the 20th century efforts of INI, (the National Indian Institute), excluded from the "modernizing" campaigns of their nation, the Maya have maintained trust in their own dignity and, more broadly, the efficacy of their traditional way of life. For both Tsotsil and Tseltal speakers their name for themselves is "the true people."

Fray Diego de Landa, the 16th century Spanish cleric, remains most famous for destroying the treasure trove of Mayan sacred books at Maní. (The bystanders wept when they saw their beautiful hand-painted books of knowledge go up in flames.) Landa believed the Maya to be devil-worshippers and had many who refused to convert to Christianity tortured. But ironically he had only praise for the sociability of the people. "The Yucatecans are very generous and hospitable," he writes in his *Relación de las cosas de Yucatan*, "no one enters their houses without being offered food and drink, what drink they have had during the day, or food in the evening. If they have none, they seek it from a neighbor; if they unite together on the roads, all join in sharing even if they have little for their own need" (de Landa 40).

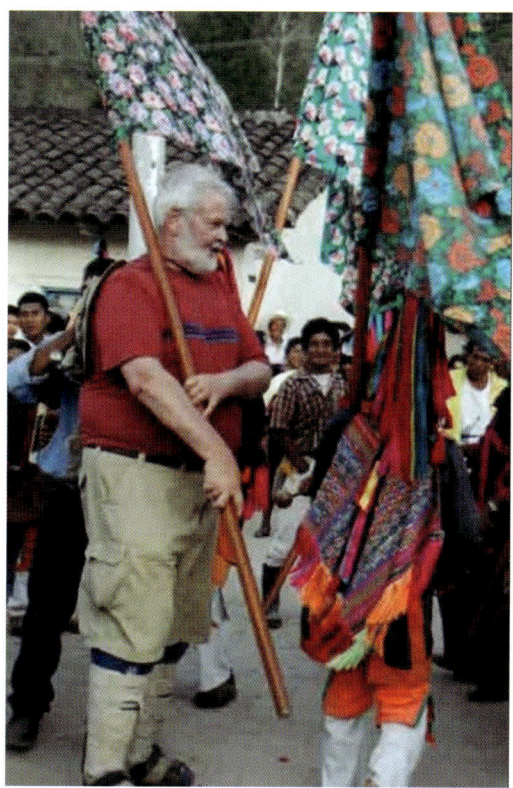

El gringo enlisted for flag-bearing and dancing with visiting Max or "Monkeys" from Chamula

Evil is coming

The Mother of Mothers we were speaking with is one of 24 players who are called the Fiesta Raisers. Their work is supported by religious officials called *Paxyonetik* or Passions with food, liquor, paint for their bodies, a place to stay during the fiesta. A recurrent troupe with some changes in the line-up each year, they represent a variety of different figures, especially on the Monday of the Festival of Games. In the case of the Blackmen, so many personages it is hard to keep track of them.

Luckily, there exists a guide to the players in the raucous entertainments of Monday. Four weeks or so before the Games at the fiesta of San Sebastián a prophesy is read out which lists the whole panoply of characters you will see a month later. (Actually the dates for the Games vary some since like Lent and Easter the fiesta is pegged to the lunar rather than the Gregorian calendar.) The warning is framed in the usual couplet style of Tsotsil prayer, here reproduced from Victoria Bricker's translation in *The Indian Christ, the Indian King* (Bricker 1981, 186).

"Many days still remain unfinished,
     Remain closed.
Beauteous work,
     Beauteous contribution
Of the festival
     Of the holiday
Of our father Jesus,
     Of our father the Nazarene.
He has seen it in his eyes;
     He has seen it in his face.
Will he still see it in his eyes
     After thirty days have passed,
Of his festival,
     Of his holiday?
He strews a bit of dust,
     A bit of rubbish

On the roadway,
          In the plaza
Of our father Apostle,
          Of our father Holy Cross.
Look now!
          Here now!
Here in a month's time
          Everything will come!
Animals!
          Jaguars!
Don't go looking for too much trouble!
          Everything will come!
They will appear here in a month's time!
          Lacandón will appear!
Blackmen will appear!
          Crossbacks will appear!
Abductors will appear!
          Evil creatures will appear,
You see.
          Danger is on its way here.
Evil is coming!
          The Turks are coming!
The French
          And Blackmen are coming!
Every possible horror is coming
          In thirty days' time!
The Turks are coming with them
          The French, everything!
Monkeys will appear!
          Lacandón will appear!
They will offer a little entertainment;
          They will offer a little joking,

They will evoke a bit of laughter
On the roadway,
        In the plaza,
They will celebrate the festival
        They will celebrate the holiday
Of our father the Nazarene."

The Nazarene?

"Nazarena" is another Tsotsil and Spanish name given the fiesta. Symbols employed which refer to Jesus include the crosses painted back and front on the Crossbacks, the red sandals the Jungle Mother carefully draws on her bare feet. The Passions, themselves named after the Passion of Christ, are financially responsible for the Fiesta Raisers' participation. But then what is the connection between the wild events and disorderly characters of Monday and the Jesus story? In her excellent ethnography, Guiteras-Holmes makes the mistake of saying the little five-day month, the *Ch'ay K'in*, or five lost days of the Maya calendar, falls at or near the time of the celebration of Christ's Passion, which is not the case. (The lost days come before Lent.) Early accounts indicate the little month originally came along in July. Did the priests and monks of the early days of the Spanish Invasion somehow manage to convince the Maya to move the lost days back five months to make them conform them with the European Carnival which precede the 40 days of Lent? This seems to me unlikely.

In the Chiapas highlands February is still fairly cold and dry. Planting of the year's corn will not begin for another couple of months, when there is at least the prospect of the spring/summer rains. To propitiate the supernaturals to assure they will get the all-important agricultural year jump-started once again certainly seems a wise idea.

Among the ancients, the Corn God died each year and was reborn the next. The end of the story of Jesus involves Him being pursued and captured by evil forces, killed and then resurrected. As speculation, it seems to me possible that a much changed and manipulated version of the Jesus story as a year-renewal tale is being enacted in the fiesta of Nazarena in Chenalho' and in many or all of the other Festivals of Games all over the Chiapas highlands.

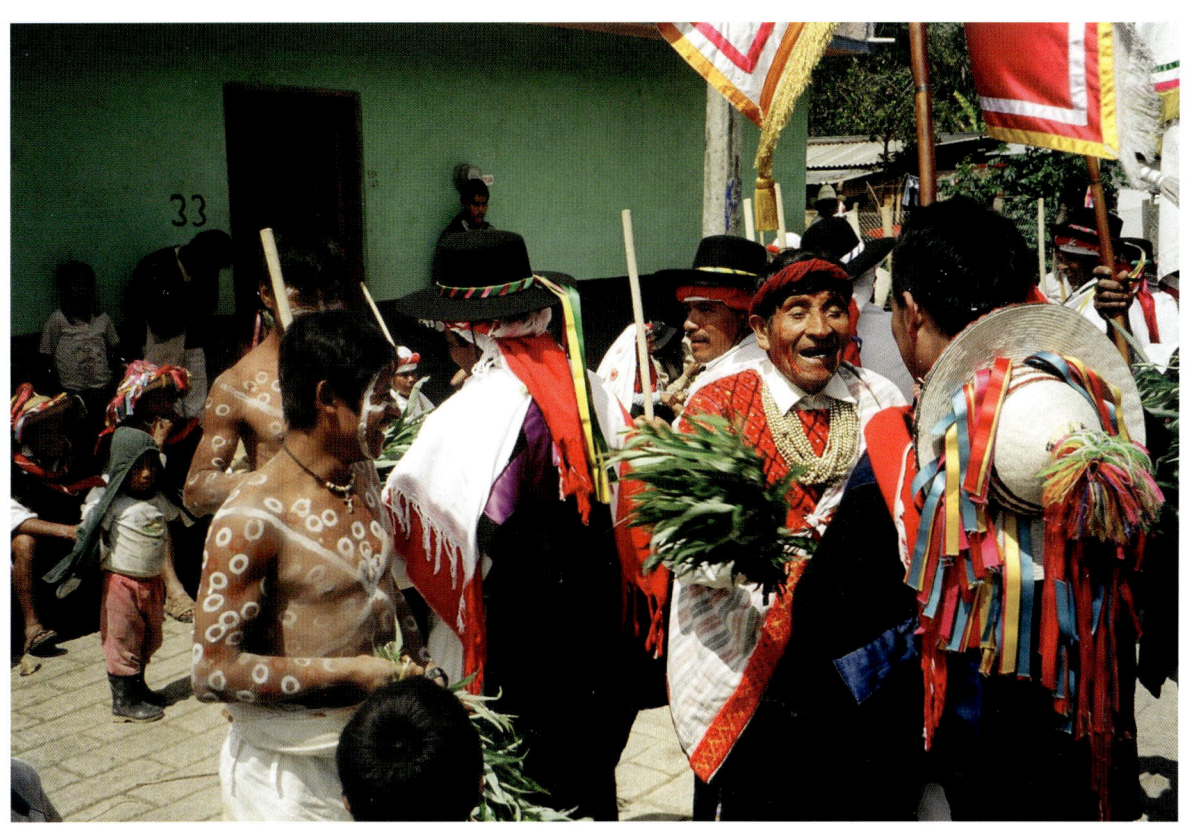

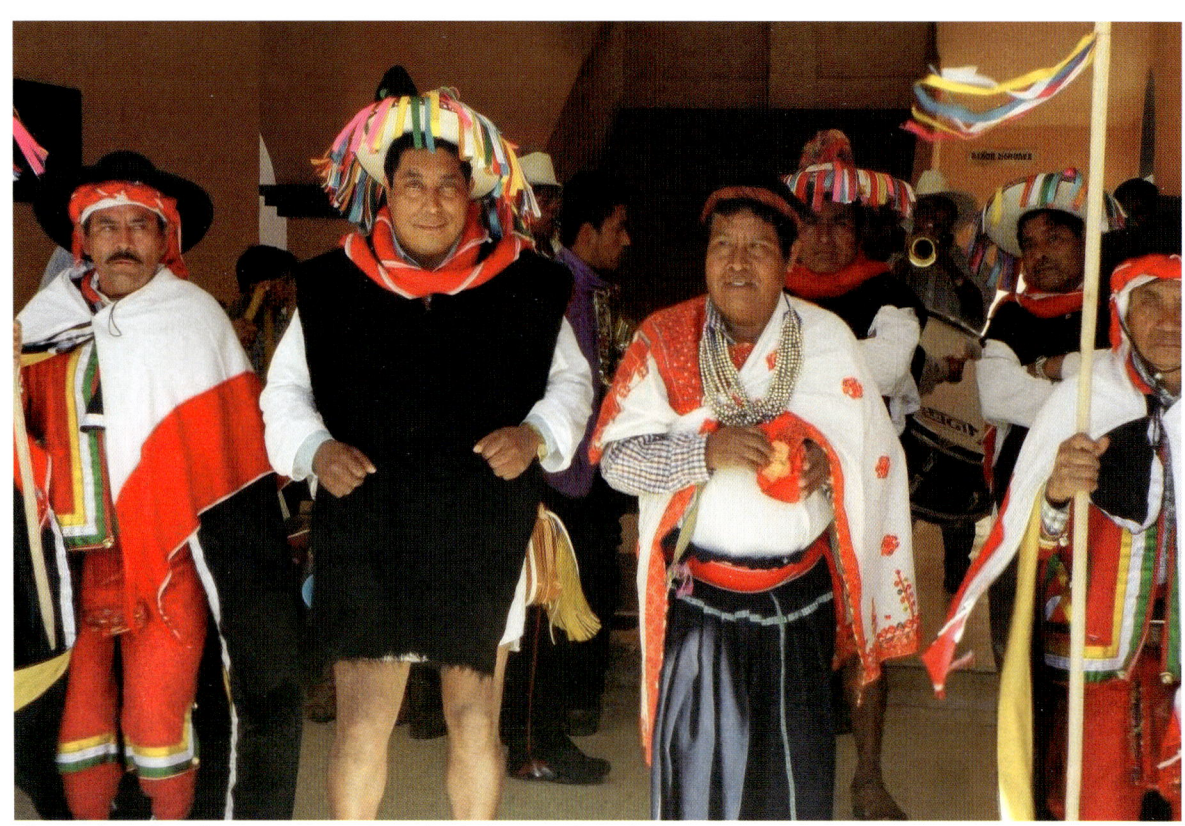

The Mother of Mothers, Passions, other officials dance at the Cabildo.

The Mother of Mothers gets dressed, Monday February 18, 2002.

Benancio must have gotten past us, because we didn't wake up until just before daybreak when we heard flute and drum going by the house. We got up, put on coats or sweaters and were out, following along after a little procession of the Passions in their ribboned hats in the chilly dark. They visited several houses, calling out to the people inside and, when they came to the door, offering prayers. To which the man or men inside responded with more prayers. Little glasses and big bottles of colorless bootleg rum with corncob stoppers came out of net carrying bags, servers poured and toasts were made, each to all, the booze tossed down in a single gulp if possible. Ámbar, Andrew, and I were offered it, accepted, fire down the throat and into the belly. In Tsotsil *pox* is akin to *poxil*, the word for medicine. Drunk early in the day it takes off the morning chill.

Some of the officials had sons or daughters along, and after they toasted, had the kids pour the liquor off into their own glass or plastic bottles. This is acceptable drinking behavior and saves you from getting so drunk you can't stand up.

At the Mother of Mother's house we were offered little squat wood chairs to sit on. A petate or woven mat was laid in the center of the room and the Mother stepped on it, got out of his wool tunic and down to men's basic long-sleeve checked shirt and wrap-around short cotton pants. While the Passions looked on, ladies brought a heavily-embroidered woman's huipil and put his head through it. Then they brought a big blue tube skirt for him to step into. Two women fussed about him, wrapping a wide red faja or belt around him, using the flat of their hands to measure out seven even folds on each side of the portion of the skirt where it flared above the faja. An embroidered white shawl was draped over his shoulders. The Mother herself wrapped a smaller rolled-up maroon shawl around her head and flicked the ends over her shoulders to hang down her back. Then they brought several shiny bead necklaces for her to put on and the Mother was ready for the day.

The Blackmen put on their makeup.

The sun is just coming up. We scurry along behind the Mother as she marches off to the house where the Blackmen are getting ready for the day.

There are Blackmen in many fiestas in the Chiapas highlands. They may sometimes represent black male slaves used as soldiers by the Spanish to put down indigenous rebellion in the 1600s and 1700s (Bricker 1981, 136), but they have other associations as well. The ones in Chenalho' are also called at various moments the "Turks," "Frenchmen," and "Monkeys," all actors mentioned in the warning of the "evil" to come in the Festival of Games. In Maya mythology monkeys were placed by the gods to inhabit the first of the four worlds they created (the monkeys didn't work out but according to the *Popol Vuh* after the gods' experiment with people made of wood failed so miserably monkeys, human-like in many ways, were allowed to stay); Frenchmen likely refers to the French invasion in the 1860s when Tsotsil men were taken north to central Mexico to fight in the country's defense [personal communication, Jan Rus]; the "Turks" may well be the *moros* or Moors of the battles of Christian and Islamic men in the medieval Crusades. Sarah Blaffer Hrdy wrote an entire book about the Blackmen of Zinacantán. In the Chenalho' Festival of Games, there are six of them and some of them also briefly portray dogs. The Blackmen are connected to the Mother of Mothers in a way I don't quite understand. Does she control or direct them? Keep them leashed in? Are they her emissaries at various times? I do not know. Could the Mother be a latter-day addition to the Fiesta Raisers? There is nothing written about her. Did she somehow just escape the notice of the ethnographers?

On the Sunday of the fiesta, the Blackmen erect two poles and string a rope across one of the streets leading to the river. They bring two live turkeys and hang them from the rope. Passions and religious officials called Captains race up and down on horseback pulling clumps of feathers out of the birds as they pass. To me, a grizzly spectacle. Once they are deplumed, the turkeys' necks are cut off and a Blackman uses one of them as a penis, passing it in and out of a circle of his thumb and forefinger to simulate intercourse and meanwhile making fun of a fictional fornicator named Andrés Luis Turkey Belly (Bricker 1973, 137). Monday the Blackmen take the turkeys around to different houses and offer them booze and stick cigarettes in the stumps of their necks, talking to the dead birds as though they are dead family members…"Oh Dad, have a drink and a drag on this butt."

Tuesday both turkeys are cut up and the Mother of Mothers oversees the cooking of a large cauldron of turkey soup at one corner of the town square. The Blackmen bring the firewood and do the heavy lifting while the Mother gives instructions and stirs the pot. I was treated once to a bowl of the soup freshly made, very chile hot and greasy. I drank it, then got halfway down the block and threw it all up in a gutter.

Over the years that I attended the fiesta, there were always changes in the cadre of the Blackmen. The majority of the players were young men, but there were several older guys involved on occasion, and at least a couple of boys of nine or ten. Their faces are always blackened but their outfits vary. Most wear white wool *chamarras* like the ones men wear in the neighboring município of Chamula. Sometimes these are puffy and white with new wool, sometimes too short and threadbare with age and much washing. Some Blackmen wear the conical, beribboned, black wool (or monkey fur) hats of the Max or "monkeys" like the ones in Chamula festivities, themselves figures of disruption, bawdiness and fun, but also with sacred connections. Other Blackmen sport deblocked and smashed-down ratty old fedoras. The oldest Blackman I saw, a man probably sixty, wore such a hat with a baseball cap over it.

At first the Blackmen were standoffish from Ámbar and me. Or you could say among the comic players they were the most committed to staying full-time in their fiesta roles. But over several years and possibly under the guidance of the Mother of Mothers, they became more friendly. (The Mother figured out rightly that I could be a willing source of cash to buy a case of cool Cokes to wet Fiesta Raisers' whistles during brief breaks in their duties.)

In the morning chill, sun still not yet up, the Passions formed a line in front of a house, the Mother of Mothers stood before them and recited a long piece of prayer to a man (a Passion?) standing in the doorway. The man recited back at about the same length. Then we went inside. The house was big, several cooking fires smoldering. *Ocote*, resin-rich pine heartwood, was brought and laid on the coals at one of the fires. Flame rose up and the ocote began giving off smoke and the smell of pitch. A comal was placed over it, tongues of fire licking up around its circumference. When the fire died down, the Blackmen removed the comal, turned it over, waited for it to cool a little, and then with great care used the accumulated soot and hand mirrors to paint their faces black.

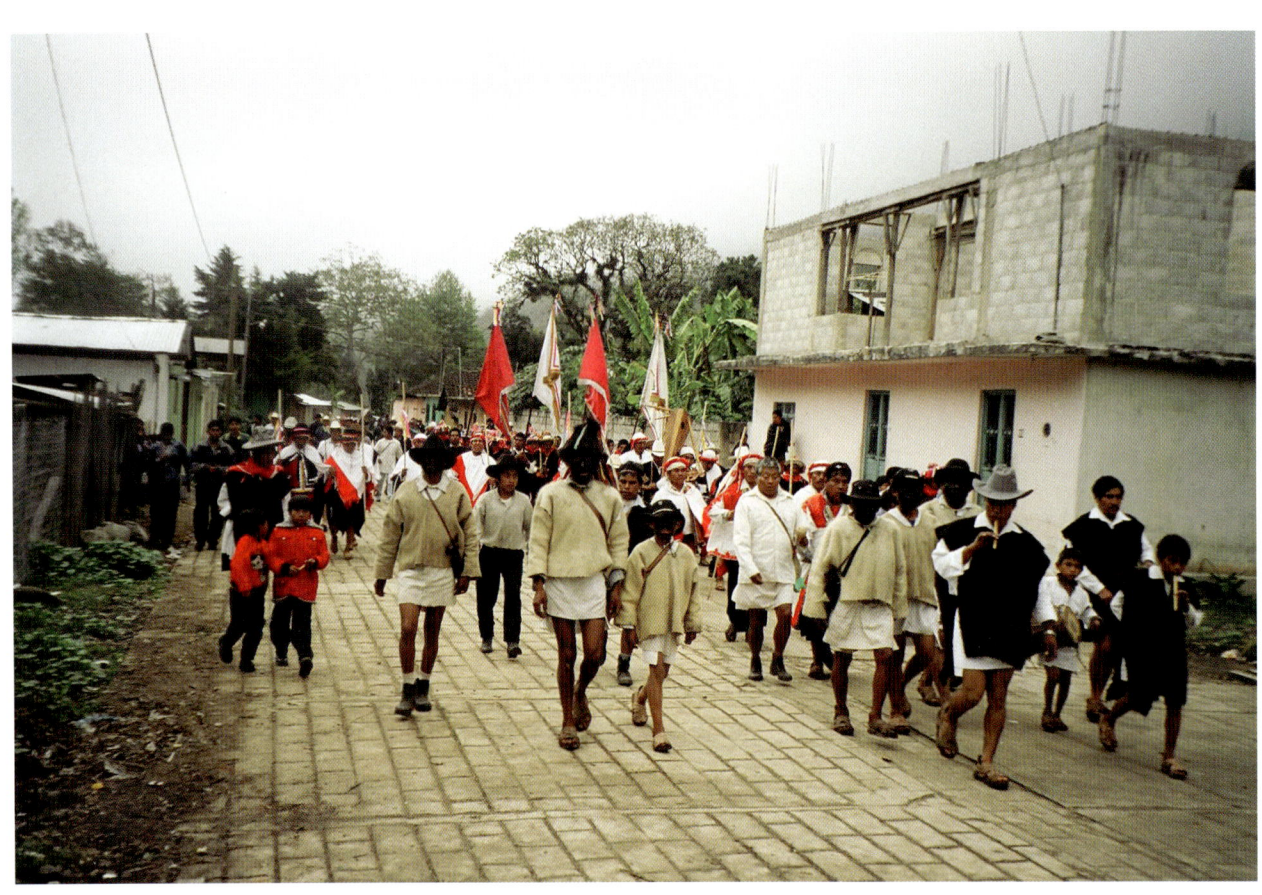

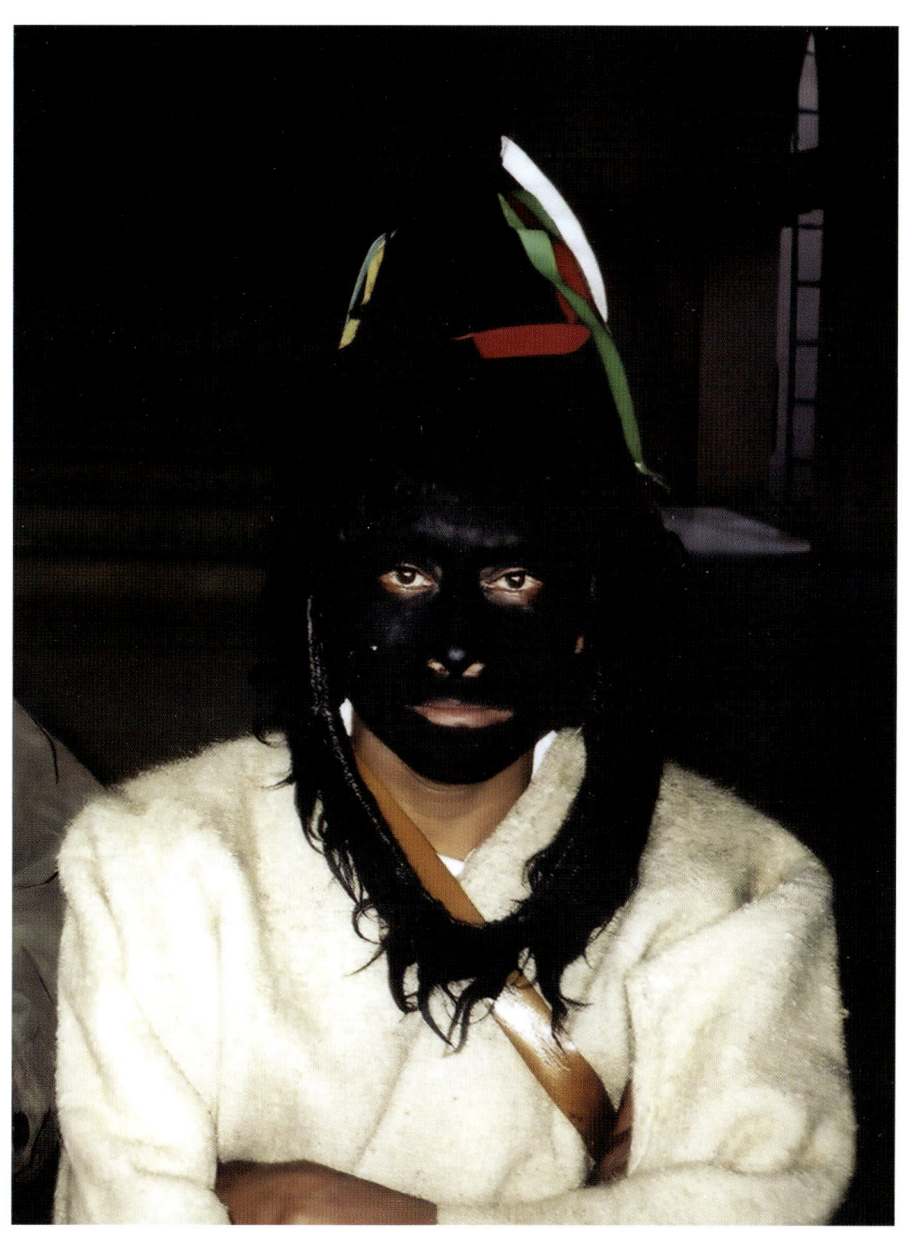

Breakfast at "It's Good"

On a street sloping down from the plaza to the river, an enterprising woman from Chamula opened a restaurant for breakfast and the midday meal. The staff she supervised were daughters or daughters-in-law, cousins, friends. I didn't see any men among them. Whether the place operated when there was no fiesta I do not know. In the outer room tables and benches, in the back one long table, a sink, a stove, a fire kept going on a raised hearth or *fogón*. A tarp spread overhead covered part of the kitchen, but the sky was visible behind it, and the smoke went up and curled and ducked out that way.

Ámbar named the restaurant the *Lek Oy*, which means "It's Good" in Tsotsil. And it was good. The menu was limited, a piece of chicken with vegetables in a soup with machine-made corn tortillas or a beef soup also with vegetables and tortillas. There was sweetened coffee with cinnamon and sourdough rolls dusted with sugar from San Cristóbal to dip into it. I think the ladies would scramble or fry you some eggs on request. Hot chilis and salt in bowls on the table. It was hard to spend more than about a dollar on a meal, and the ladies were consistently jolly, trading remarks with the customers, joking about how happy they were to be making money. When Ámbar asked the woman in charge who was the owner of the place, she tapped her chest and said *"Ho'on,""*Me," and laughed.

Becoming friends with Ámbar Past was a matter of great luck for me. She was a poet and a book designer and the founder of the small press and gallery called Taller Leñateros which produced award-winning books and a magazine called *La Jícara* and beautiful posters, address books, and cards on paper made in the workshop. Our friend the photographer Marcey Jacobson called Ámbar the most creative person she had ever known. A judgment hard to disagree with.

When I first knew her Ámbar still represented herself as being a runaway housewife. In the early 1970s she and her husband moved to San Francisco where Ámbar worked as an artists' model, writer of sayings for fortune cookies, and kept house, cooked, cleaned, did the wash. When that soured, she took off alone for Mexico. Fairly soon after she landed in Chiapas she went off to live in Magdalenas, an extremely poor and removed municipio to the north of San Cristóbal beyond Chenalho'. Beginning with almost no way to communicate with women who took her in, she slept on dirt floors and in corn cribs, sickened with fever, had an appendicitis and nearly died, recovered, and after a year spoke Tsotsil.

Through her friendships with older women seers and curers she learned traditional stories, songs, magic spells, prayers, myths, and beliefs which no other outsider had heard. At the time Ámbar first invited me to go along to Chenalho', she was finishing the essays for a book of Maya women's prayers laid out and presented as poems called in Spanish *Conjuros y ebriedades* and in English *Incantations*. I was lending her some mild editorial assistance, mainly listening while she carefully shaped her thoughts before writing them out. Learning some of what she knew about Tsotsil women's culture exhilarated me. (In Ambar's own generous description, she calls me her co-pilot while she was bringing the *Incantations* in for a landing.)

Over the years, she attended the Festival of Games in Chenalho' 44 times. When she invited me to go along it was in a friendly, open way, but I felt also Ámbar had some kind of wonderful surprise for me up her sleeve. At that point had I told her about my failed project concerning Maya transvestites from the mid 1990s? I'd received funds from the U.S. Social Sciences Research Council to study the differences in meaning between dressing as a woman in a highland fiesta and a man living female in village Yucatán. The comparison was a good one, in one case no implication about the man's sexuality in daily life, in the other crossdressing as clearly an advertisement of the man's homosexual desires and practice. The project failed because it turned out to be much more difficult and needed much more time and fieldwork than I could give it or that the grant would support.

Painting the Crossbacks

After breakfast, we go to find the gentleman who portrays the Jungle Mother. He is not at the house he is using for the fiesta. His wife says he's already out painting up his two assistants, the Crossbacks, so we set off and find them on the main street not far from the town market.

"Jungle Mother" is my own perhaps clumsy translation of the Tsotsil *Me'kabinal*. In her books, Victoria Bricker calls the figure the "Lacandón Woman," noting that historically generations of male rebel leaders in the Lacandón jungle of Chiapas had the title or name *Cabnál* or *Cabenal*, which is close to current Tsotsil *ka'binal* or *ka'benal* [Victoria hears the word slightly differently from the way I do]. In Zinacantán fiestas two male religious officials portray *ka'benaletik* whom people speak of as being Lacandón (or jungle) people (Bricker 1973, 48-9).

The Jungle Mother is older than the Mother of Mothers, taller and less fleshy. He is in his 70s and amazingly sturdy, luckily, given the amount of leaping and running around he's going to do today. When he has time to talk with us from moment to moment he goes back and forth between being apparently preoccupied and serious and bright-eyed and making jokes. At the same time both welcoming and elusive, open and hard to know. I sense some kind of jolly or bemused other-worldliness about him.

(Some years later Ambar and I and her friend Saideé Suárez made up an expedition to go visit the Jungle Mother. His home was up a dangerous, poorly graded dirt road out of the settlement of Polho'. It was a heavily-clouded day of off and on spitting rain, but he was off working one of his cornfields some way away. The women of the household sent a boy runner off to get him and set to work preparing a chicken soup from the groceries Ambar had brought. But then the boy brought back word that his grandfather had decided not to break off from work to come home. The women insisted we stay until the soup was ready and we could eat together.)

Today we find the gentleman soon to become the Jungle Mother still in his men's clothing on the entrance street to town where a table has been set up and some benches put out. One of this year's Crossbacks is a middle-aged man and the other an adolescent, both already stripped to their shorts. Men coming running with plastic buckets and bottles of liquor and fermented sugarcane chicha. These they lay out in two carefully equal rows

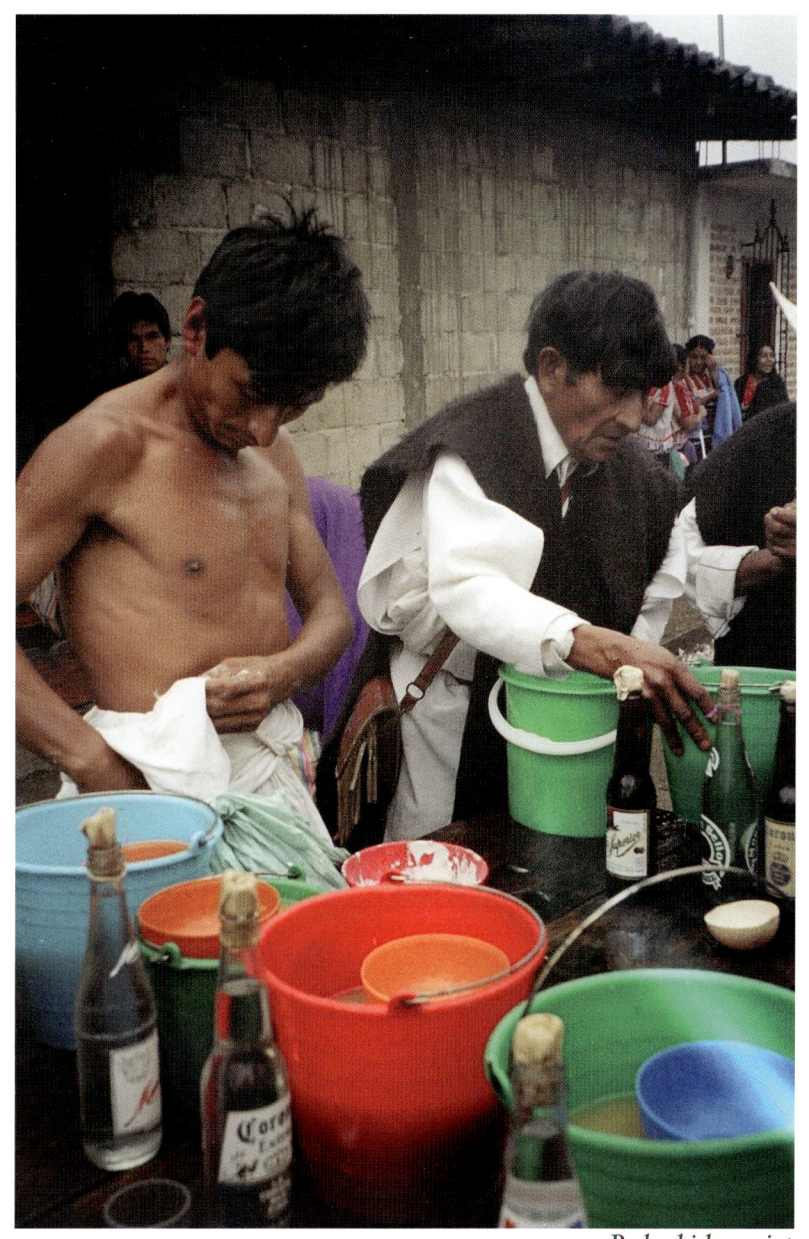

Posh, chicha, paint

on the table with shot glasses and small gourds for drinking. Two of the buckets contain a white paint paste which is a mixture of corn flour and water. The red in the other buckets is mixed from ground-up seeds of the annatto bush (*Bixa orellana*) and called achiote. Combined with garlic and other spices in small bricks as achiote paste for dishes like *cochinita pibil*—Yucatec oven-roasted pork—it is readily available in Mexican markets near me in central California. Annato was used by the ancients as paint for their bodies and to cover the stucco walls of many of the temples of the Maya cities. Even exposed to the elements, the dye has a long life. Swatches of it appear on temple walls or bas-relief statuary more than a thousand years old.

(I do not know it as a fact, but I suspect the provision of the paints and the pox and chicha for the three performers are the responsibility of the Passions.)

While the crowd of men and boys watch, the Jungle Mother first paints a cross and then one large "X" on the back of each of his assistants and the same thing on their chests. Then he uses the lip of a Coca Cola bottle to plant red and white circles all over the Crossbacks' bodies. They do some of this work to one another. Finally the Mother carefully draws a "mask" on their faces in white. (He himself will paint a similar mask of the red annatto on his own face.)

Controversy over what the circles are about. Most likely they indicate the Crossbacks have connection to jaguars. At a museum in Tuxtla, the state capital, I remember an example of a kind of sack garment from the Lacandón jungle made out of scraped bark and covered with circles which represent the wearer as a jaguar spirit. On the other hand, in pre-Invasion Maya iconography human figures appear covered with spots which seems to indicate they are diseased. And in the 1940s a Crossback showed his circles to Calixta Guiteras-Holmes as markers of infection (Guiteras-Holmes 1946, 166).

The same assistants who brought the paints and the liquor also come running with six tied bunches of weeping willow leaves which the Crossbacks and the Jungle Mother will carry all day and at one point use to bless and "cleanse" civil and religious officials, and at another to wake up some sleeping Blackmen.

Once the Crossbacks are all carefully painted up, the liquor and the chicha on the table offered to all present and consumed, the men sing in an open-throat way (la-la-la but no words), the crowd disperses and the Mother goes off to the house where he and his family are staying to dress.

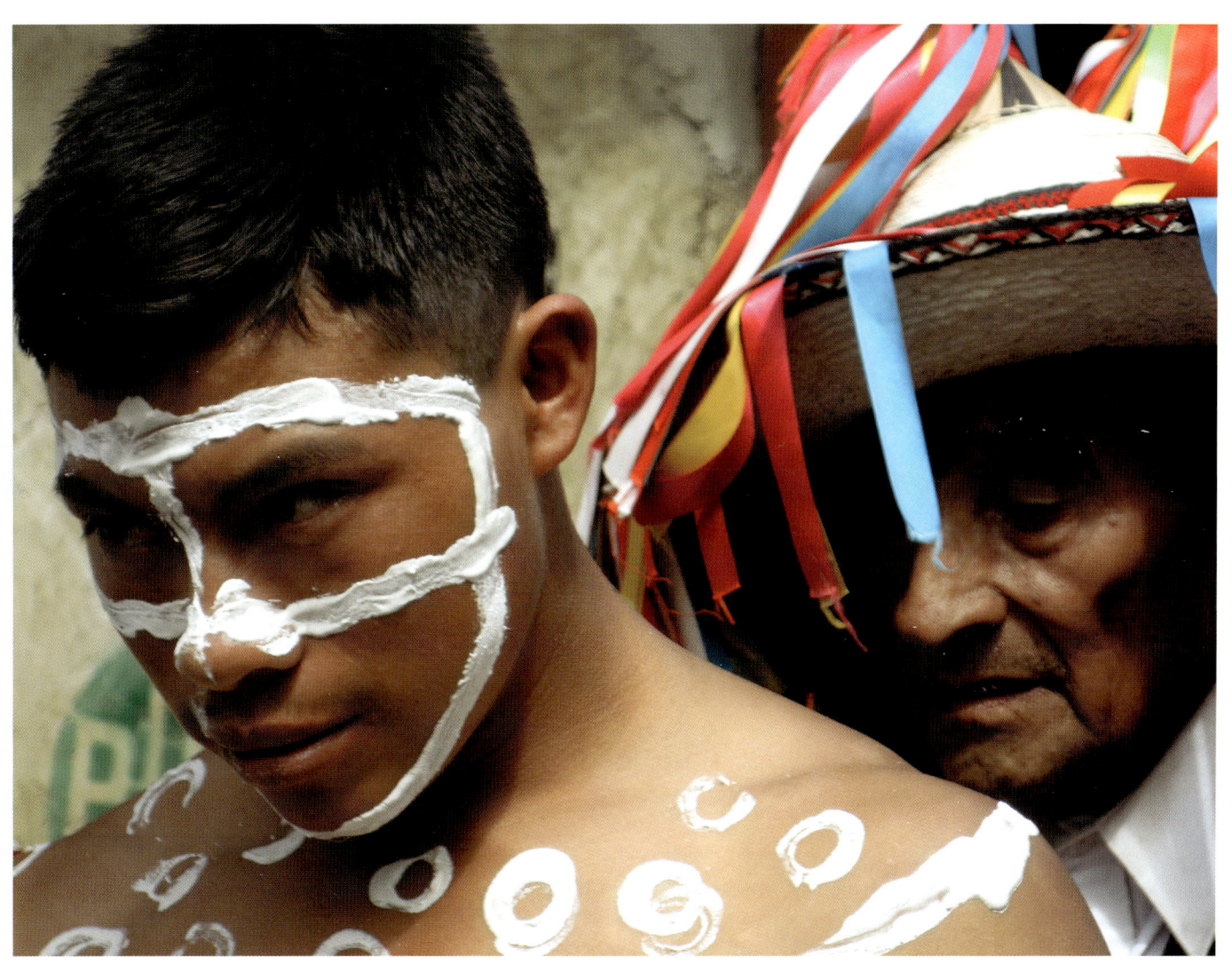

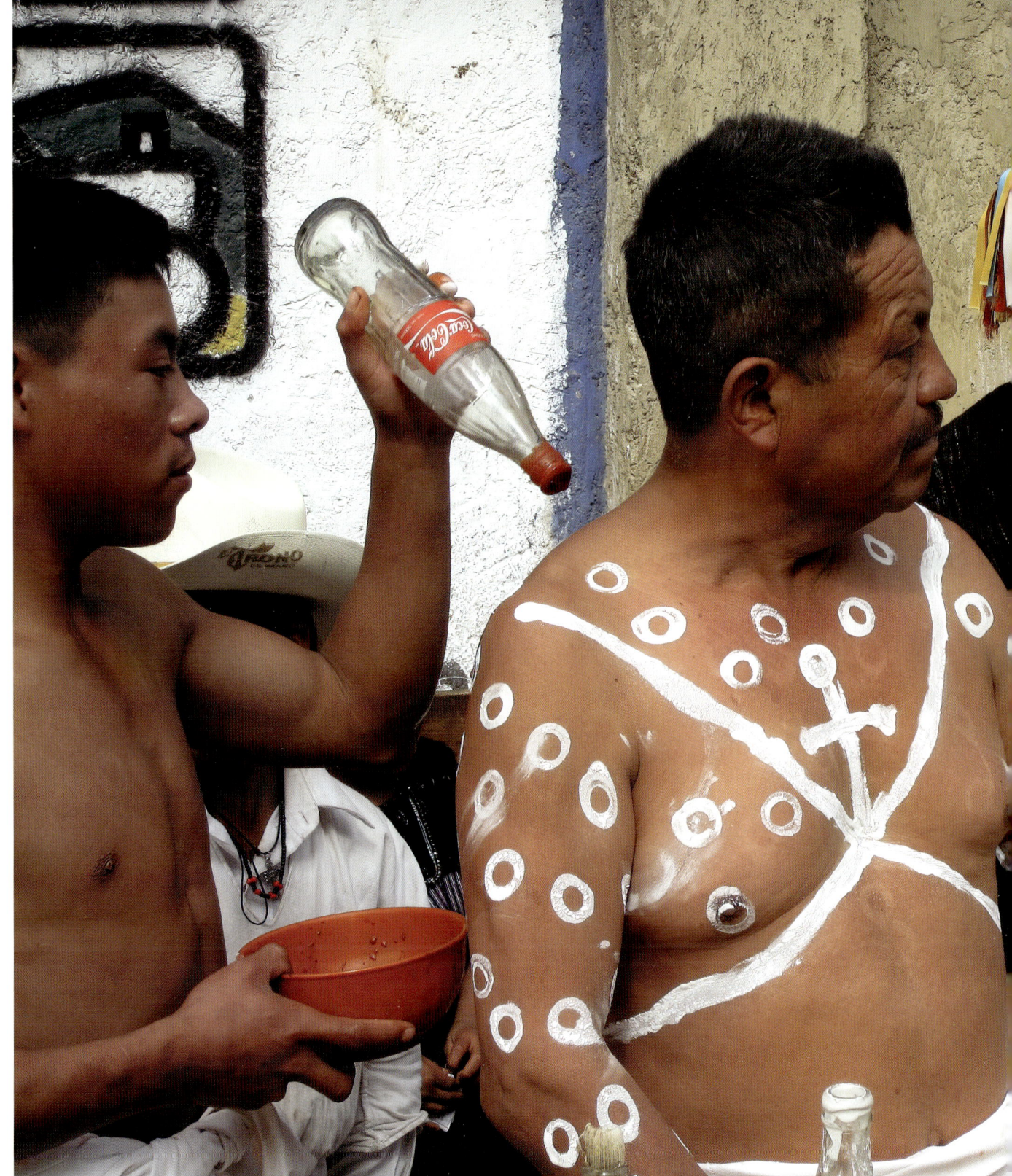

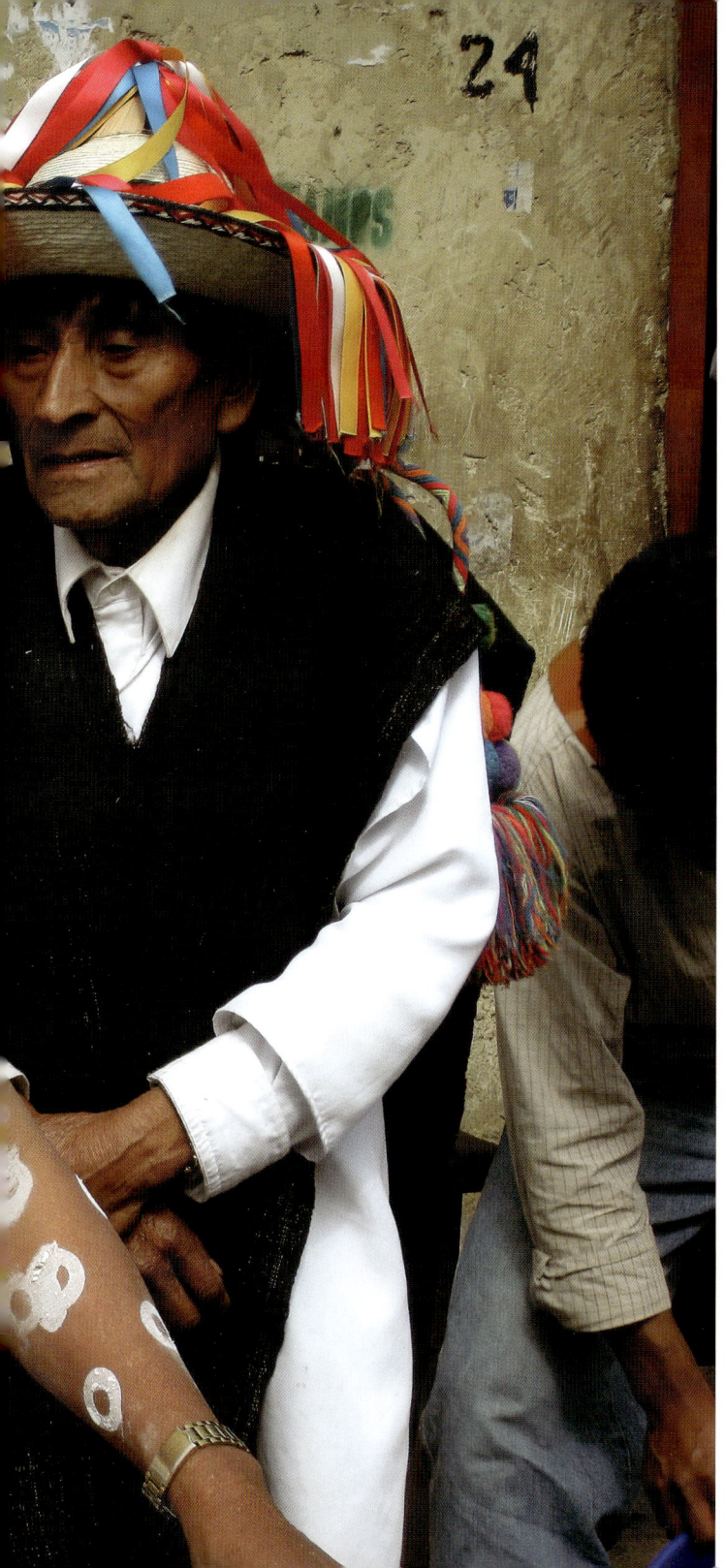

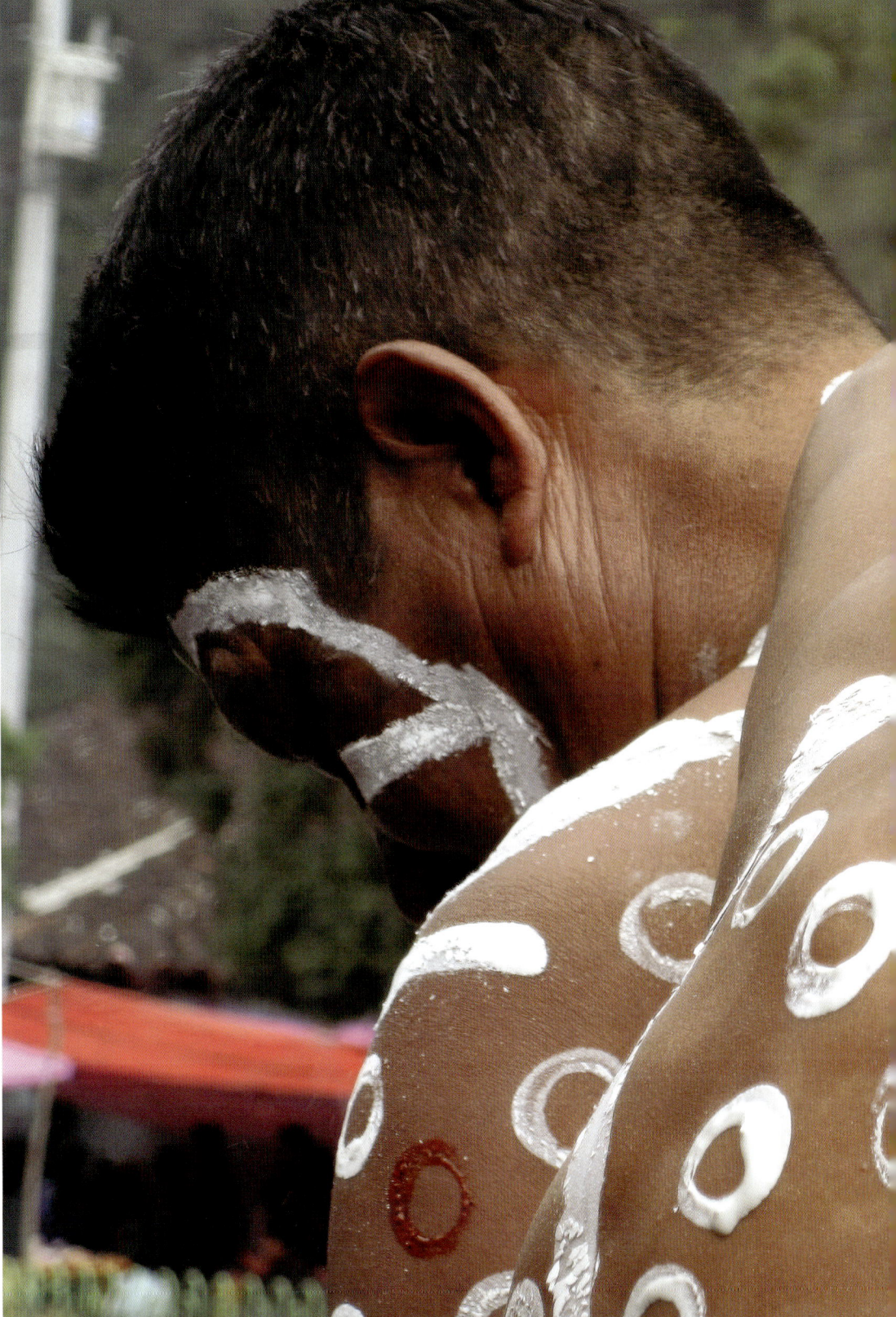

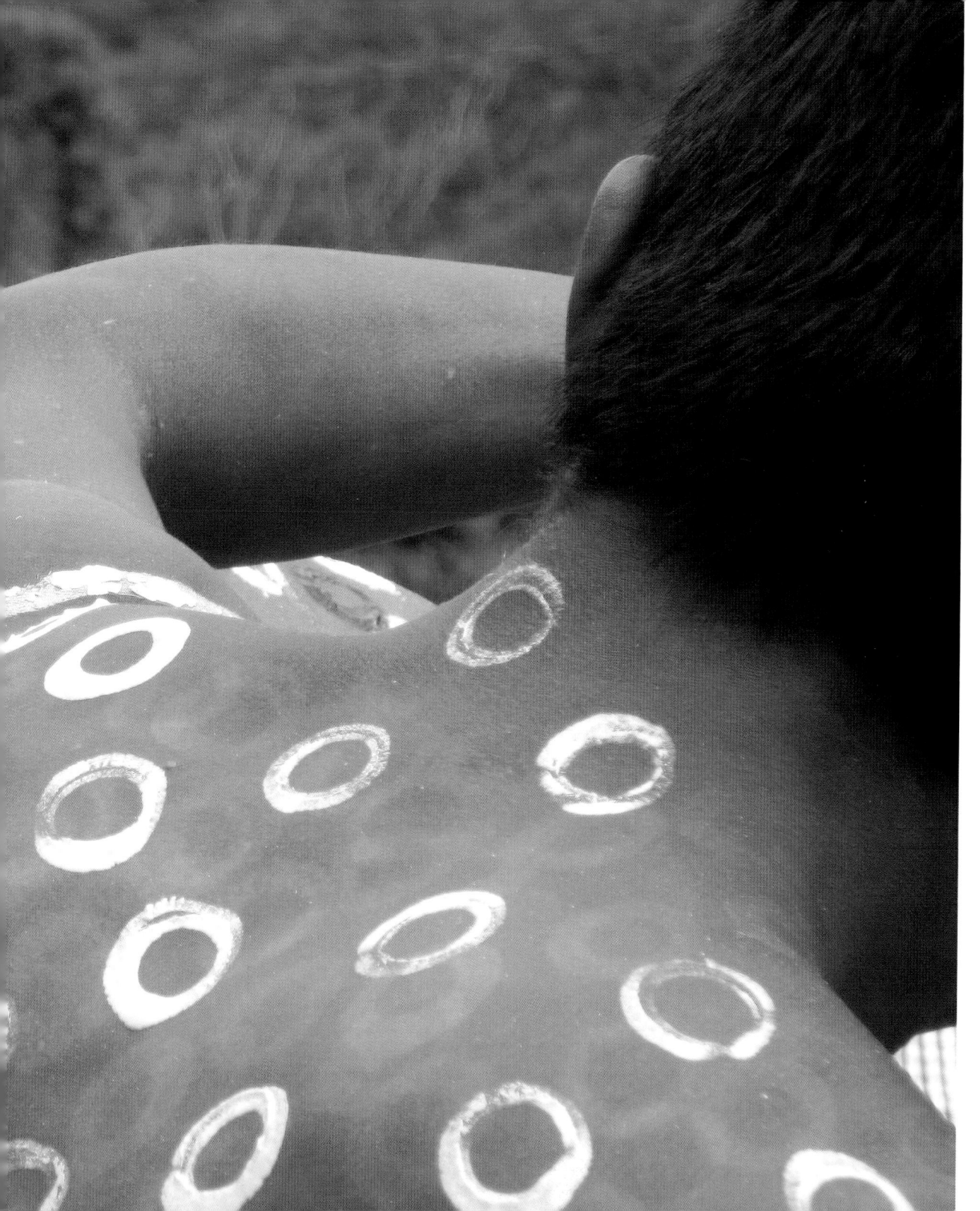

The Jungle Mother's Sandals

Back at home, the Jungle Mother puts on a heavily embroidered huipil and over it a knotted machine-made shawl with embroidery around the edges, a blue skirt with red faja and huge beautiful hanging pompons.

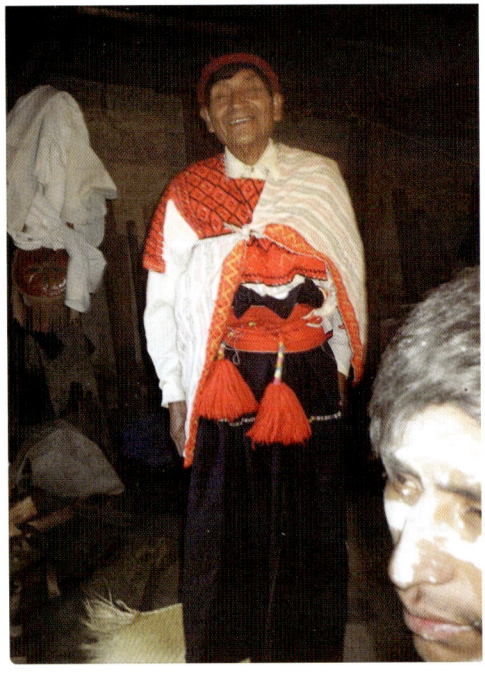

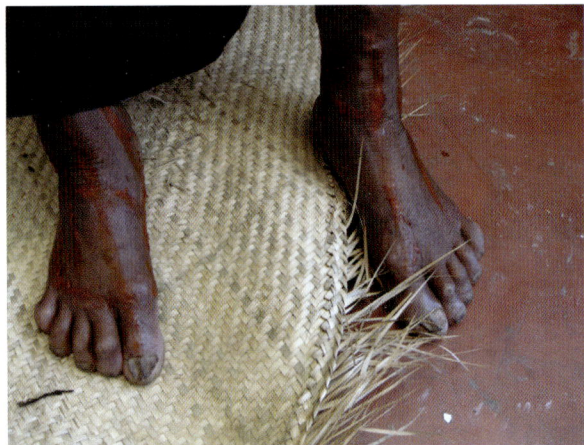

Then the Mother sits on a small chair to paint red lines on her feet with the same annatto used for some of the circles on the Crossbacks.

She tells us the sandals she paints represent the ones Jesus wore. But as she charges about town all afternoon barefoot the painted sandals and (possibly) the annato mask she paints on her face are the only visible references her get-up bear to "The Nazarene."

There is also no Passion of Jesus enactment in the fiesta, no actor struggling to bear a cross with men in Roman legion outfits beating at him with toy scourges (a pageant still performed on Good Friday in Watsonville, California, near where I live). But if in fact Nazarena is a year-renewal fiesta, the few key references to Jesus may be enough to indicate His death and resurrection are being represented, though without narrative. (This is particularly likely if Jesus is still associated in any way in people's minds with some version of the corn god of old.)

The variety of characters a single actor can represent and the changeability of symbols the fiesta staff employ are reminders of the differences between our ("westerners") ideas and those of Maya people. Regarding time, for us events usually occur in sequence or one direction. This first and then that. "Progress" is a doctrine based on forward movement. Maya time is less strict, often circular, time doubling back on itself. The birth of the father of the Hero Twins in the *Popol Vuh* comes after the appearance of the boys, as translator Michael Bassett points out (Bazzett, xiv). The Yucatec *Books of Chilam Balam* written in Mayan during the colonial period often mix (western) historic with Pre-Conquest events and myth. In Mayan time things happen over again, or everything seems to be happening at once. The Blackmen of Chenalho' come from myth, but also from wars in the Middle Ages, and from the 16th, 17th, and 19th centuries. Fiestas take place in linear time (dates you can put on a calendar) bur also in circular, annual time.

As with time, so with symbols. In classical western painting objects tend to telegraph a single meaning. Saint Lawrence bears a griddle because the Romans roasted the Christian bishop over the fire for making fools of them. Saint Cecilia, patron of music, often carries a musical keyboard or a stringed instrument. In the Maya fiesta one-to-one correlations between object (or actor) and meaning don't always exist. The Jungle Mother portrays a lady who appears in a creation myth but also reminds us of Jesus through the red annatto sandals. Such overlaps are difficult if you want correlations to be one-to-one. Clusters of meaning attached to one thing may be hard on the western mind.

Dancing women

Around midday on Monday the oompah band hired by the town strikes up, the bells in the church tower begin to toll and the religious officials' assistants hoist up some of the saint figures and bring them out to be paraded around the town square. A figure of Jesus makes the tour as does Santa Lucia, whose bearers are women. The procession is led by two "bulls" dancing along with the firecrackers along their backs not yet lit. Skyrockets and women with smoking pots of copal incense, many spectators gathered.

The third of the major transvestite actors on the Monday of the Festival of Games is The Abductress. I know very little about her. She has two attendant gentlemen in red outfits and turbans, both of whom carry long thin planting sticks. Collectively the three of them are called The Abductors. The Abductress takes part in the procession of saints, dancing along the street shaking rattles in time to music of harp and violin by players following her. She also takes part in her own version of the Ceremony of the Mat that the Jungle Mother participates in, but I've never seen her version.

In the procession also a group of men and boys called the Dancing Women. They are the ones who sing "*O'lol-antson, o'lol-tsebun,*" or "I am half a woman, half a young girl." All of them sport fine examples of traditional women's clothing and men's ceremonial ribboned hats. Some have water-filled balloons stuffed in their blouses to give them large breasts and many now wear sunglasses. They also have rattles to shake and their own harp, guitar, and violin-playing musicians. There are times when they dance before the saints in the church. The Dancing Women do not belong to the Fiesta Raisers. They seem to me less official performers whose motives are partially devotional (amusing or pleasing the saints), but also just having fun partying. (If this is true, they are like the "unofficial" Max or "monkeys" in Chamula, who have no stated fiesta duties and are dressed up and acting wild for the pleasure of it.

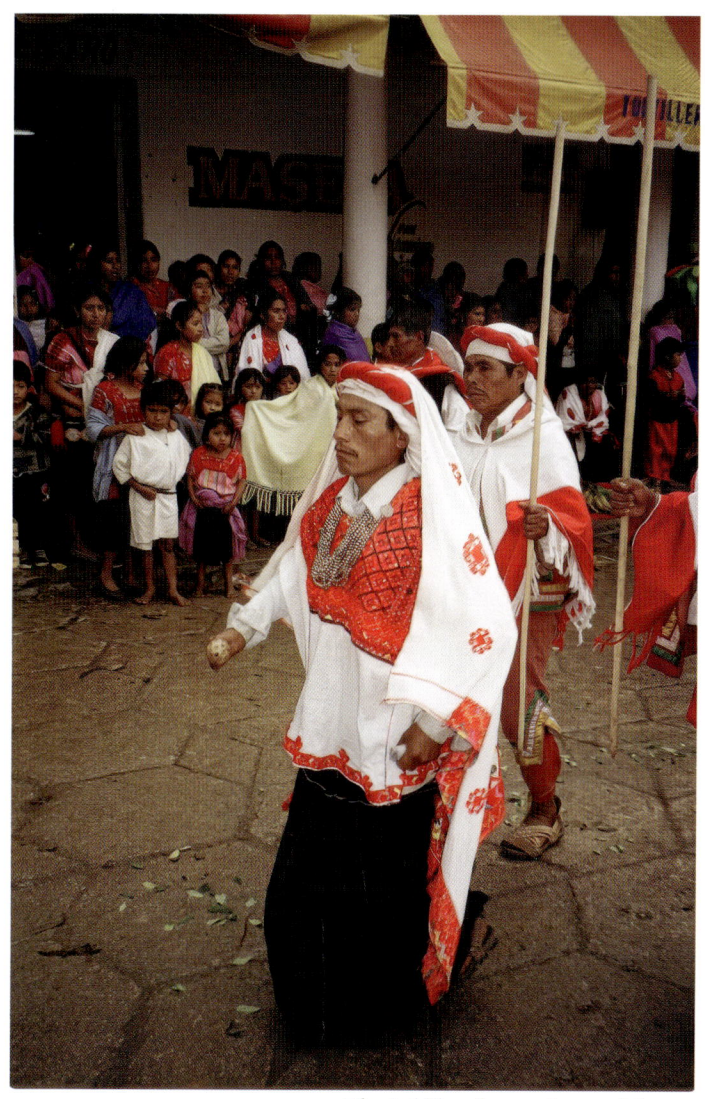

The Sak'il and an assistant abductor

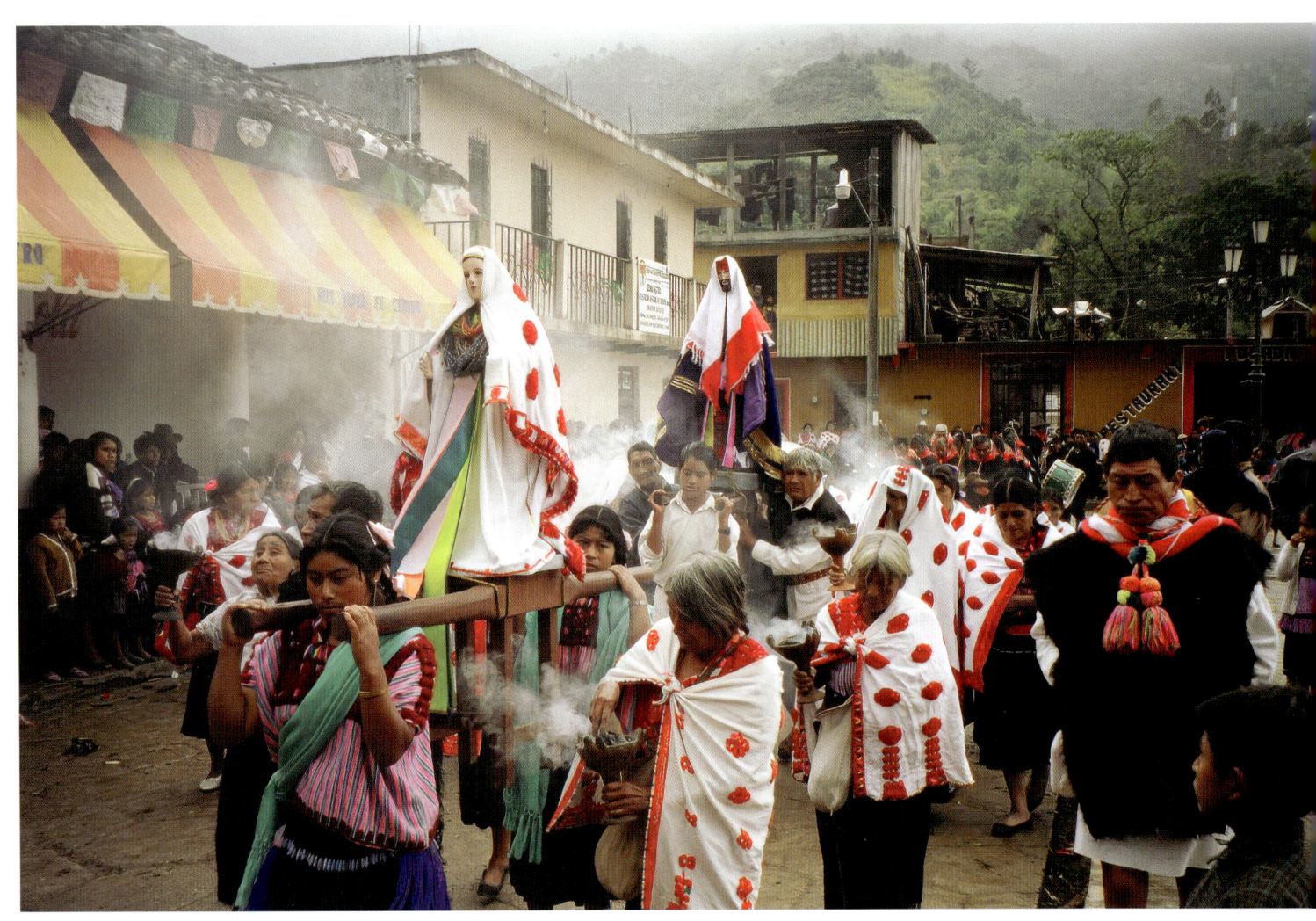

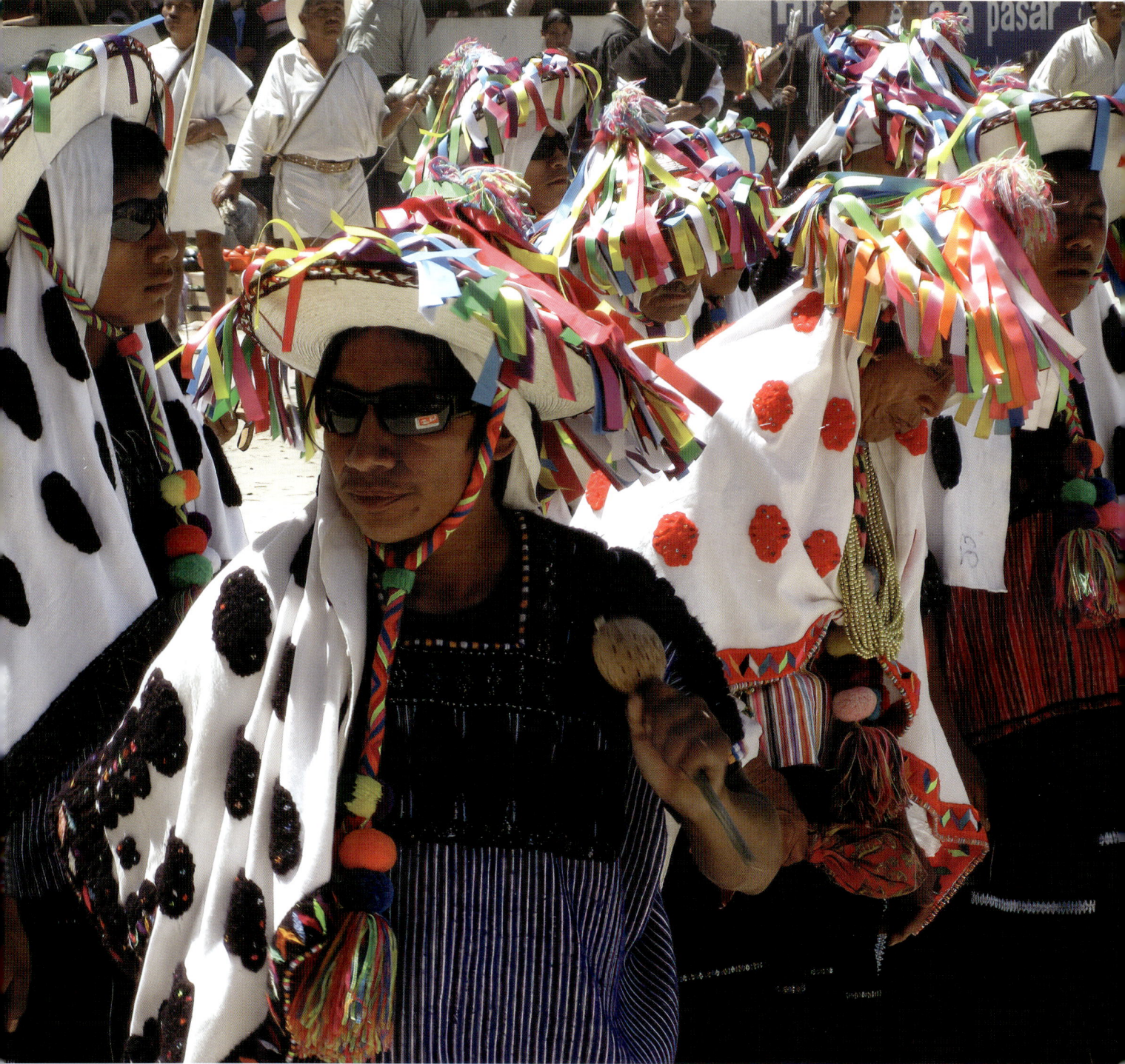

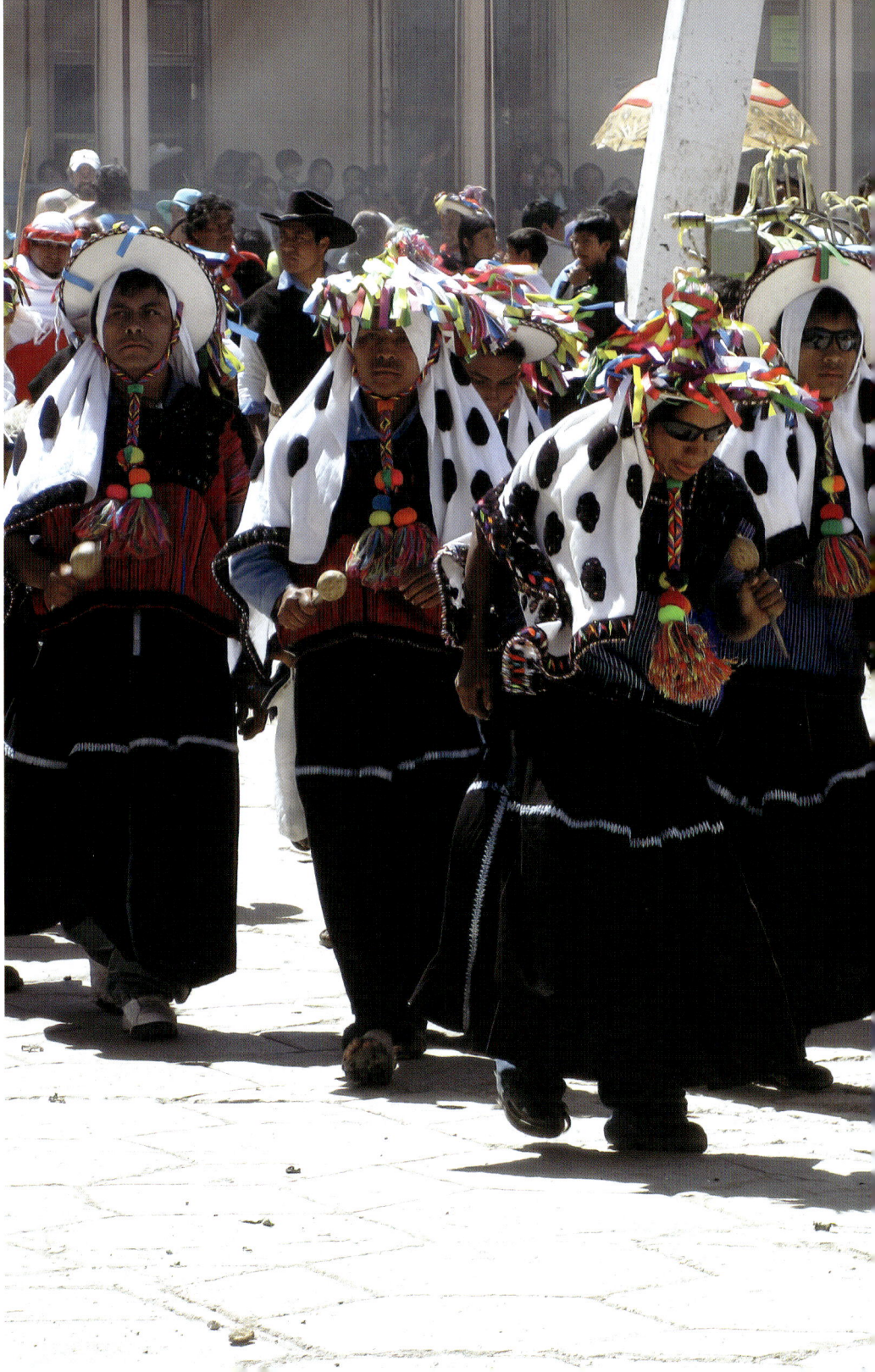

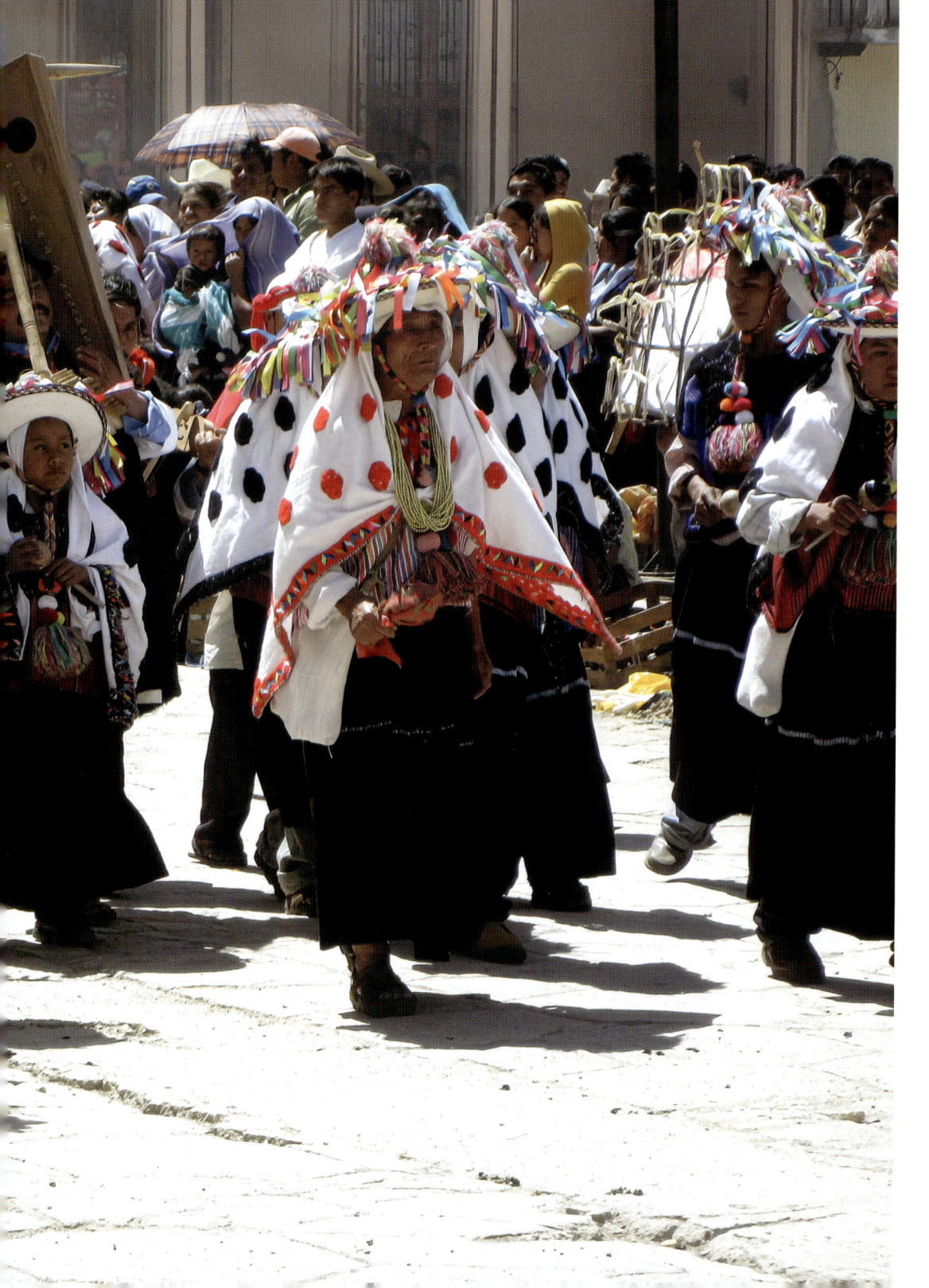

"The saints feel cold as we do"

People think of their saints as being like human beings possessed of super-human powers. They act in the world for even higher beings, God, Mary the Mother, and Jesus. The belief about the saints is similar to the Spanish-speaker's view in the saying, '*Si Dios no quiere, ni los santos pueden.*' (If God doesn't want it, even the saints can't do it.) The saints can grant favors, heal sickness, perform miracles, but above all they protect us. People go on pilgramages to thank them for past signs of grace. When Loxa Ernandes, a seer and ritual singer from Chamula, came to the Festival of Games with us we made a special trip up the steep hill across the valley from the church so she could light candles and pray on her knees before the altar in the chapel of the Santa Cruz (the Holy Cross, which is considered one of the saints). When Loxa was near death as a small child her mother came there to pray for her. Loxa survived.

In exchange for their interventions the saints want themselves properly celebrated. Parades, skyrockets, incense, new vestments, food and drink given away freely. If the religious officials stint in their generosity—if there is not enough of something—the saints will notice. Rain coming during the fiesta is a clear sign of their displeasure.

Ideally, you sign up for religious *abtel* or "work" or in Spanish a "cargo" or burden because a saint has come to you in dreams and asked you to "carry" him or her "for a time, for a year" (Wilson 1973). Very much as humans or gods in the ancient glyphs are bearing time—the years—on their backs.

The film we made in 1966 in Tenejapa, "Appeals to Santiago, was built around prayers of an *Alperes* (*alferez* or "ensign") and a *Martoma* (*mayordomo* or "majordomo"), both principal actors in the fiesta of Tenejapa's patron Santiago (Saint James). The recitations are in typical Mayan couplets where the ideas rather than the line-end sounds "rhyme." To me they speak of the intensity and depth of feeling people bring to their dealings with their saints:

Alperes:

"Holy sir, Captain Santiago
Holy sir, Apostle Santiago,

Your captains come to you
To celebrate with our hands
To celebrate with our feet
With our mouths to the ground
We come to ask for life for our bodies
To offer drinks to Santiago
To pour a glass in his honor
To wet our lips for his holy service."

Martoma:

"True saint, Mother *Jalalme'tik*
I am bringing my candles to you
I have prepared myself to serve you
During the days of Santiago
For a time, for a year I carry you
Your sacred vestments
Your sacred things."

Alperes:

"We are four holy seniors, four holy guides
Our younger brothers are together
Our hands are washed, our feet,
Our bodies are now together
To meet the saint on his holy day
Thirty, thirty-five, our holy candles are sixty
Sixty our holy gifts.
Now it is done, they have gone from us
Gone to beg for life for our bodies
The bodies of all of us, our wives, our sons
Gone to protect us from sickness

They go from us, our sixty gifts
Our sixty candles."

Martoma:

"Holy Mother Jalalme'tik
Holy Patron San Alonso
Apostle San Pedro
Master Santiago
Your holy workers come to dress you
We come to bear your holy body
To show you your town
To show you your people."

Alperes:

"Now it goes from us,
Now it happened
Respected Father Santiago."

Martoma:

"We come to ask for life for our bodies."

Alperes:

"We come to enjoy your holy hour."

Martoma:

"We are not dirt
We are your servants who come.
To beg you to keep us in your sight
To ask you to keep us in your heart."

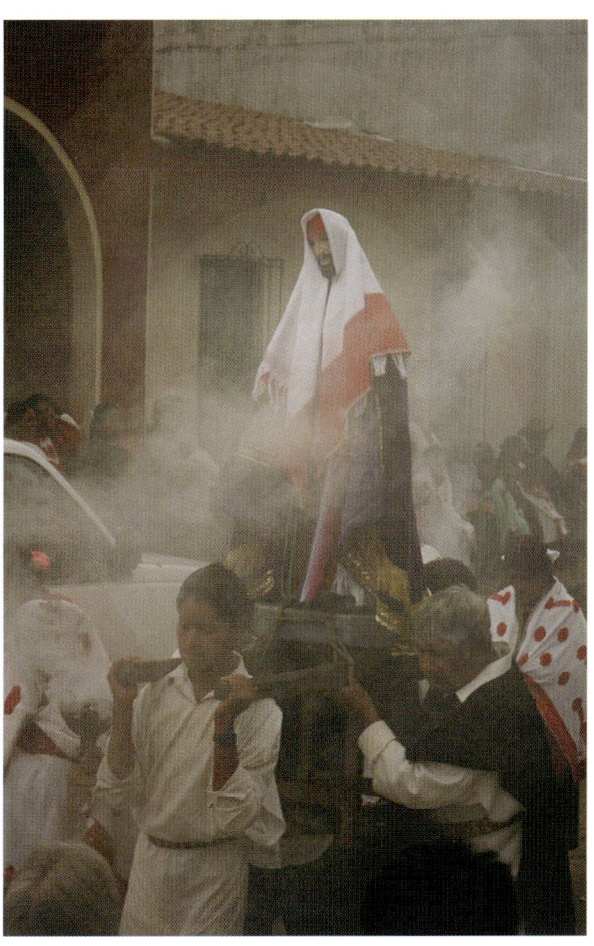

The Guatemalan Woman

While others are processioning about the square, a mysterious woman is going through the town market "stealing" small items from vendors and putting them in her basket, all under the watchful eye of several "soldiers" in uniform carrying toy wooden rifles. This is the Guatemalan Woman, the fourth of the major men in skirts. She is also involved with one or both of the *toros*, bulls made of a wooden cage covered with matting, a man inside, and firecrackers set to go off consecutively along lines of a complicated series of fuses. Fifty years ago, the actor was called *La Ranchera* or the Woman Rancher. She is the kind of fiesta character whose "meaning" changes with changing times. Thus, previously it was dominating *ladinas* (rancheras) who lorded it over indigenous people and robbed or cheated them in commercial dealings. Beginning in the late 1970s, however, large numbers of Guatemalan Maya fled across the border into Chiapas to escape the genocidal massacre conducted with impunity by the Guatemalan army. At one point, there were 400,000 of these refugees in the state. At first, Chiapas Maya people did all they could to feed and house their Guatemalan brethren. But then some went back to their homeland, and others got integrated into Mexican society. No matter where they are really from, women who work in prostitution in southern Mexico often claim to be from other Central American countries. Men in Chenalho' have most likely encountered such women, and thus the change in the fiesta character seems to be an updating of a female figure who cheats indigenous people.

This kind of replacement was noted by anthropologist June Nash in the Tseltal town of Amatenango, where a straw figure burned on Good Friday was once the traitorous disciple Judas, but over time migrated into being other bad actors (for example for a time he was an oil prospector, suspected of trying to rob the town of a resource rightfully theirs).

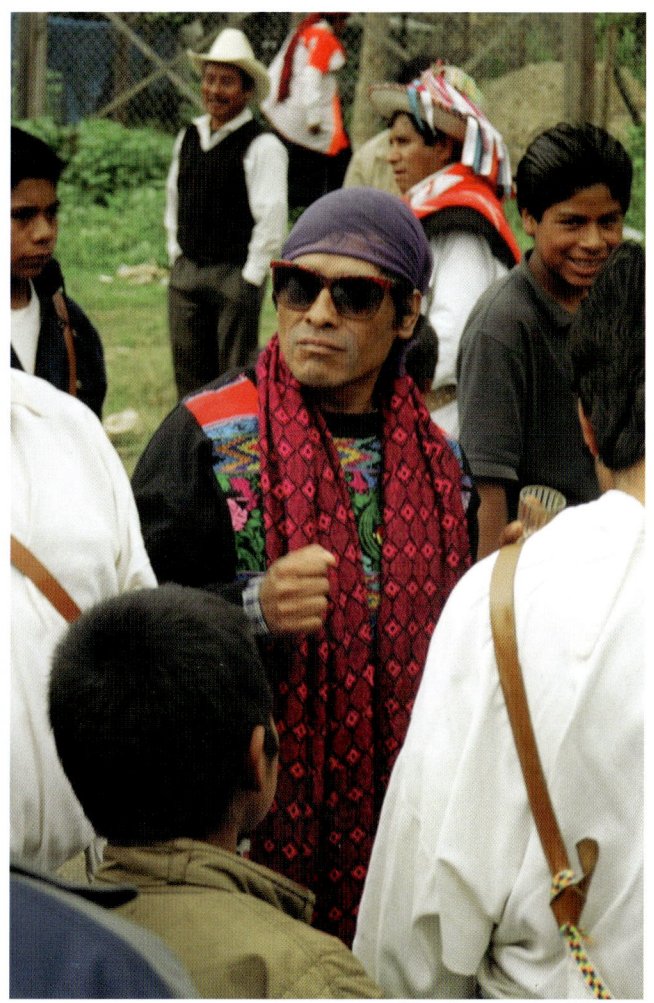

The Guatemalan Woman

Ritual healing

After the procession of the saints, the religious and civil officials come marching along and gather at the Jungle Mother's house to beg her to come forth. The Blackmen are nowhere to be seen. The officials line up in a tight formation and the Mother and the Crossbacks run circles around them one way while the two Abductors and the Lady Abductor and the Guatemalan Woman with her soldiers and her firecracker bull circle in the opposite direction.

Then the Jungle Mother and the CrossBacks hear confession: "Do you have an illness?" the Mother asks the official. "Yes, Mother, I can't get it up anymore," he jokes. "Well I have the cure for that. Here, I'll bless you with my branches and you'll get hard again soon enough." She crosses her branches and sweeps them several times over the chest of each official to cleanse and restore him.

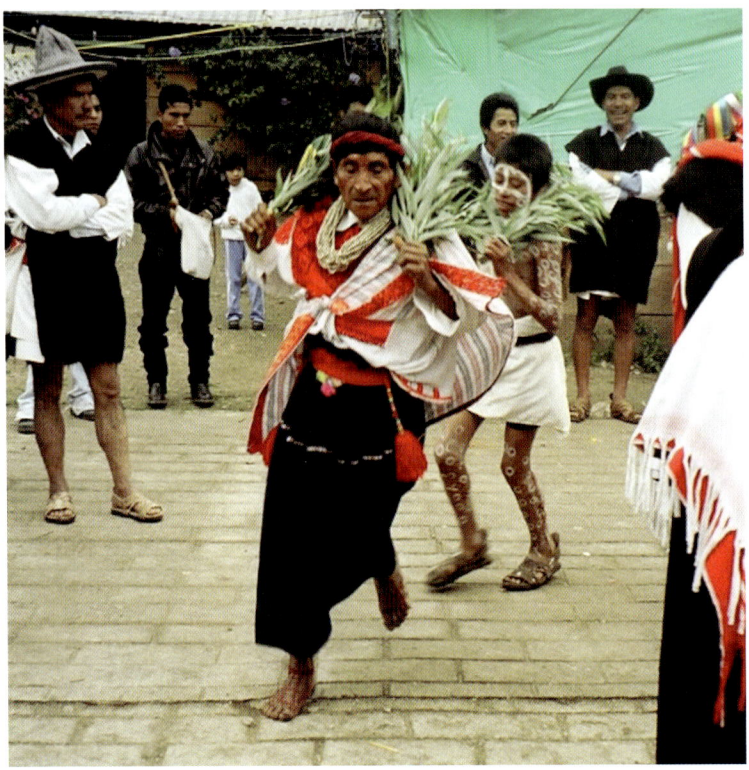

Jungle Mother and one of the Crossbacks

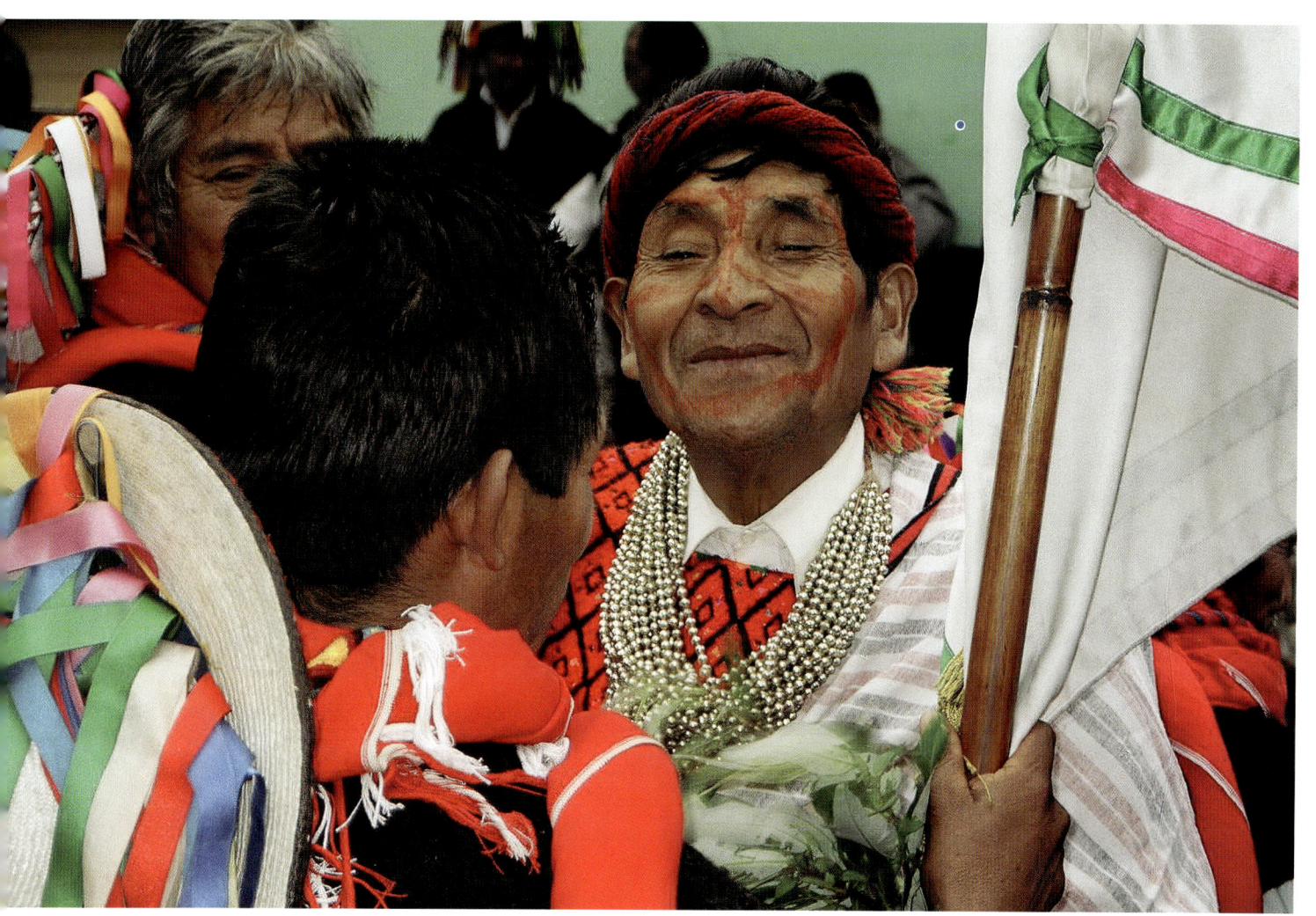

Jungle Mother hears confession.

59

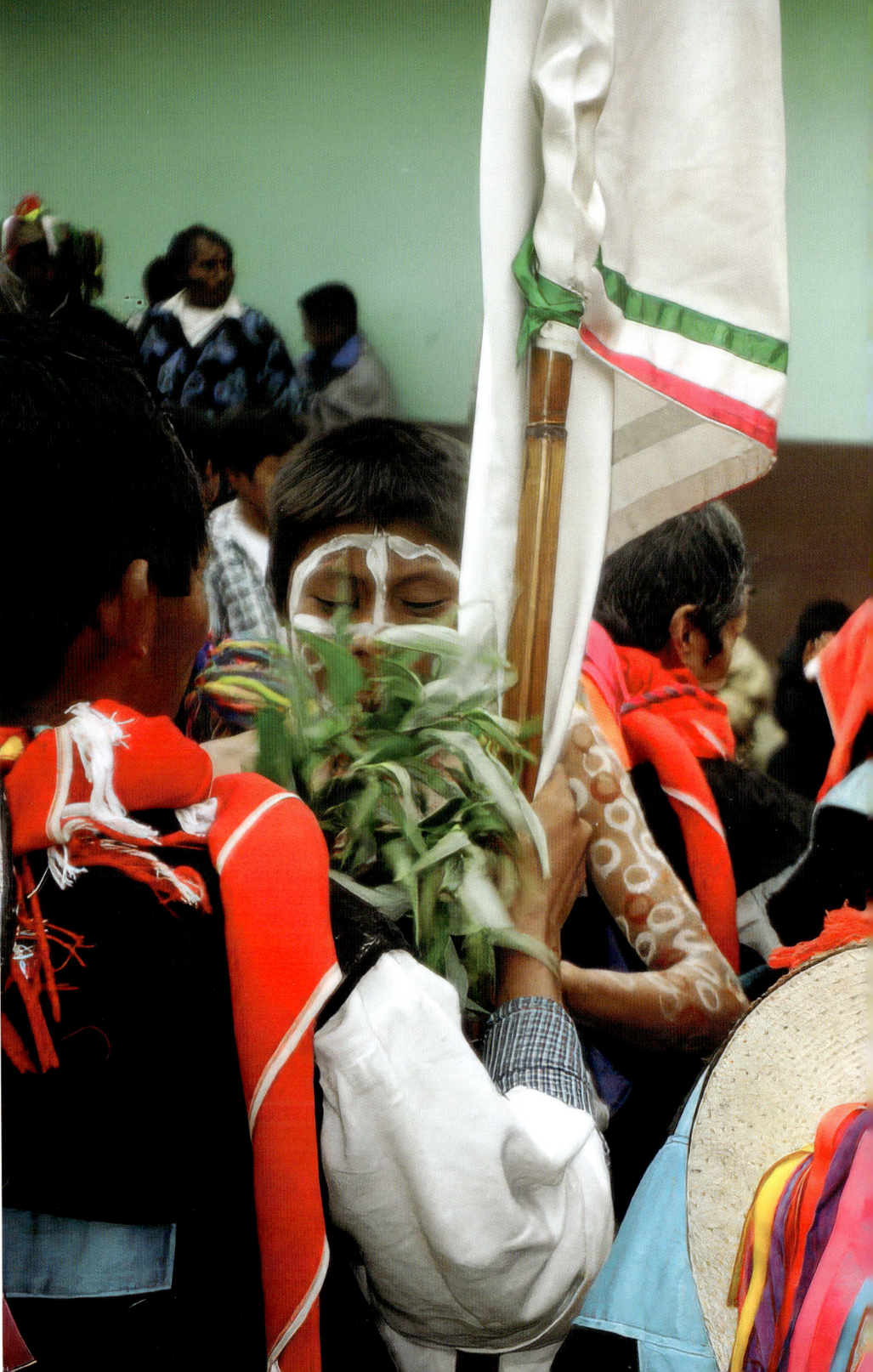

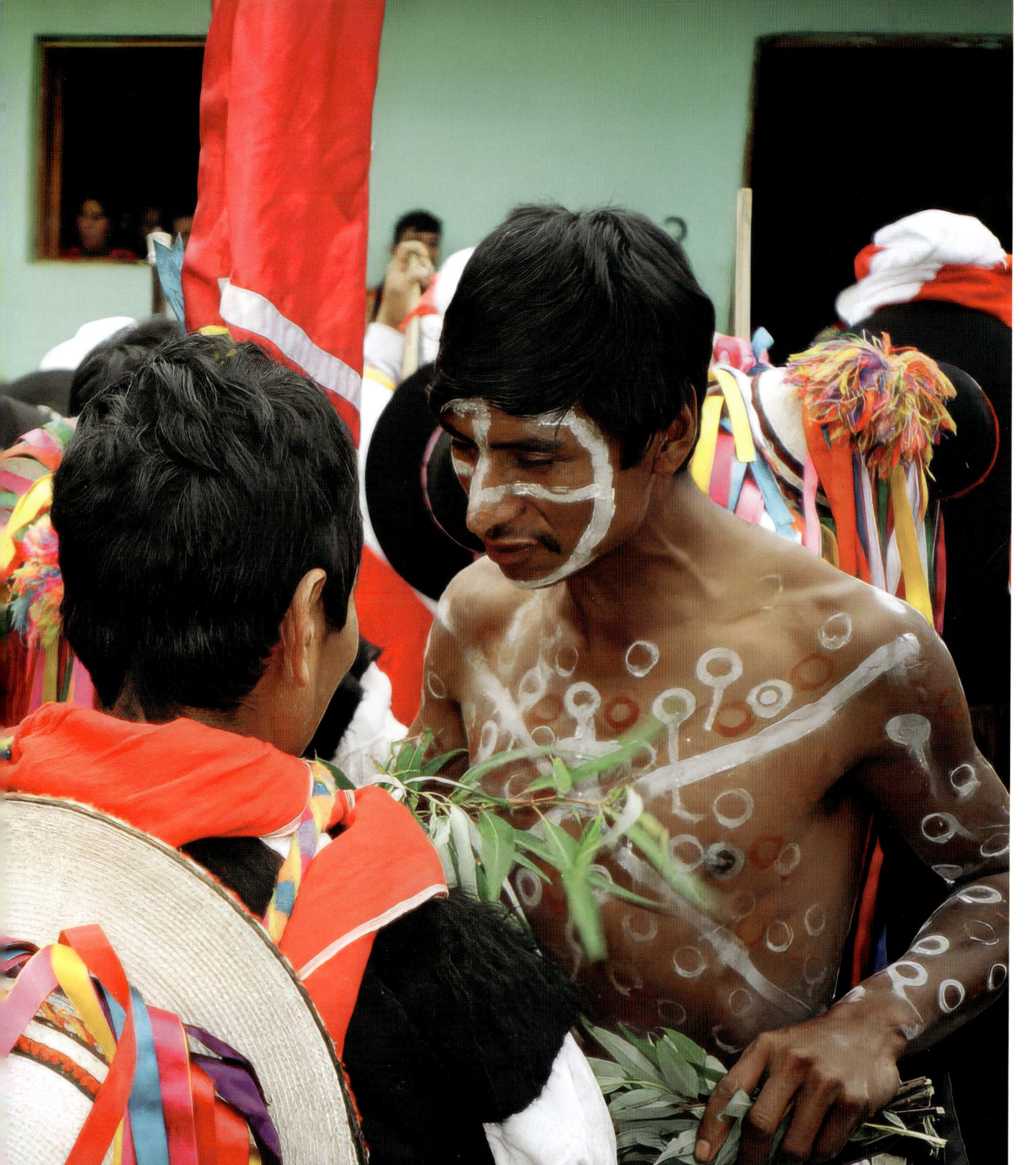

Back in the plaza, one of the bulls' fuse is lit and as the firecrackers and spinners begin to go off, the bull dances, spewing smoke and flame. A man pretending to be a matador waves a jacket instead of a cape before the burning figure. Is he part of it, or just drunk? I don't know.

The Blackmen show up with lassos they mean to use to capture the Jungle Mother and the Crossbacks and the Abductors and the woman Abductor.

The fugitives come on the run, the Blackmen lay their ropes down on the cobblestones but the Mother, the Abductress, and their entourages jump over them. They circle the plaza again and now the Blackmen are lying in the street in pairs, toe to toe. But all six of the fleeing characters jump over them and manage to escape.

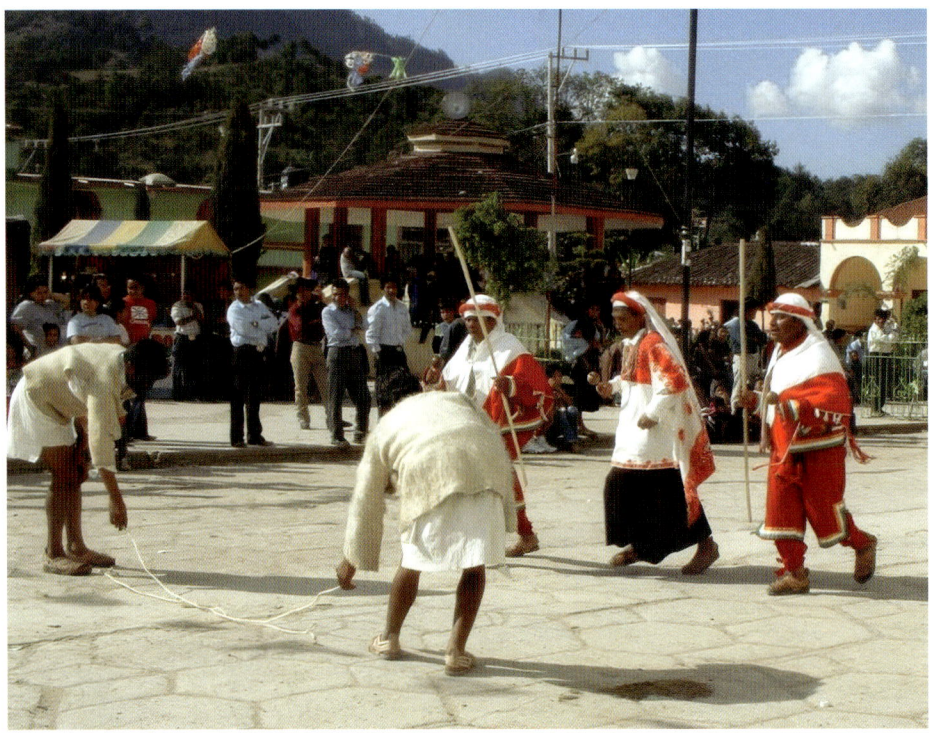

Abductors jump over the Blackmen's ropes.

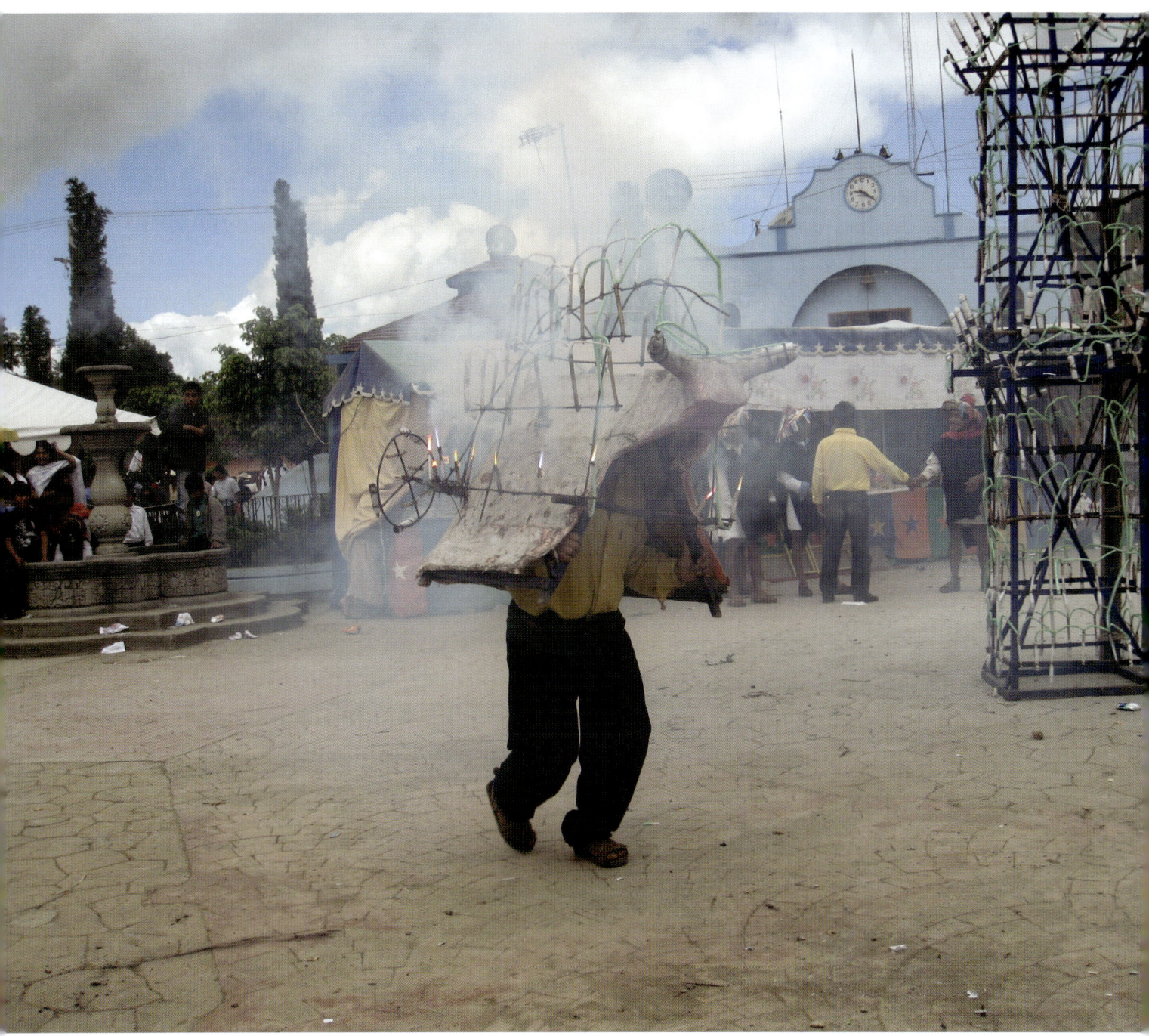

Rolled up in a mat

Jungle Mother and her Crossbacks seek refuge in the house of one of the Passions. They get down and hide under a straw mat and pretend to go to sleep. The drama at times called "Rolled Up in a Mat" begins.

Three Blackmen come and pound on the door and force their way into the house.

"Passion!" their leader cries. "What's this crowd doing in here? What is it you're hiding?"

The Passion's advisor, called the BoozeMeasurer, answers, "Nothing…these people just came to visit…just family and friends in here."

"Well we're looking for my aunt. She's missing! And if she stopped by here, if she begged something to eat off you…just tell me how much you want and I'll reimburse you for it."

"No..nothing like that going on in here, sir."

"Oh, there must be…" says the head Blackman. "I'm going to have to send out my dogs, big ones, to have a look around. And they have really big noses, so women, girls, you better cover up your cooking pots…don't want my dogs getting their snouts into your secret places you know!"

Hunched over and barking and sniffing, the other two Blackmen circle the room snooping, grabbing small children, growling at the women. Widespread laughter.

Back at the straw mat the Blackmen dogs start digging and scratching—

"There's something under there!" says the head Blackman, "something smelly…something like my aunt maybe! Have you got a planting stick so I can dig around and see if she's under this mat?"

The BoozeMeasurer claims to have no stick, but then the Blackman borrows one and inserts it under the mat and works it back and forth in a suggestive way. "Better step back…out of the way of my big stick here, Mr. Passion. You don't have dynamite to blow up this rock under here, do you? It's really hard, this stick won't go in.."

"Sorry sir, I don't--"

"Well then I better see can I just lift this cover…"

And he pulls the mat off and forks it up into the rafters, causing a snowstorm of soot to come swirling down.

"Whew! That came off easy, didn't wear me out at all! And look there! My aunt and those wild men, asleep. And since they're just lying there, we better apply our new rule to

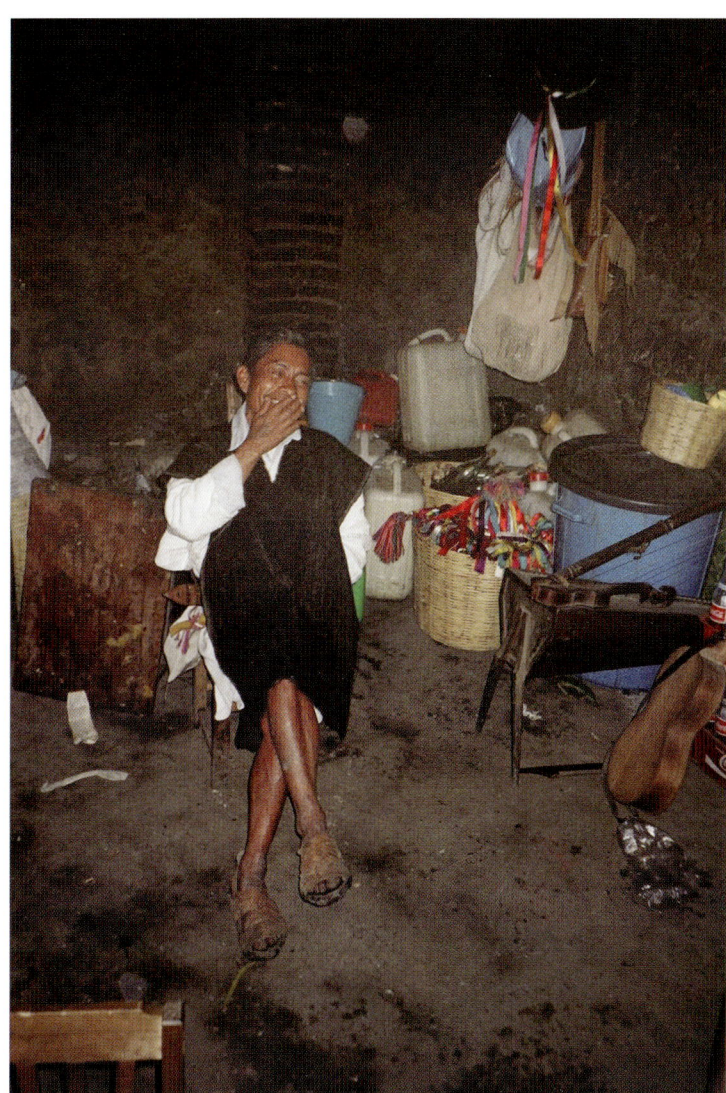

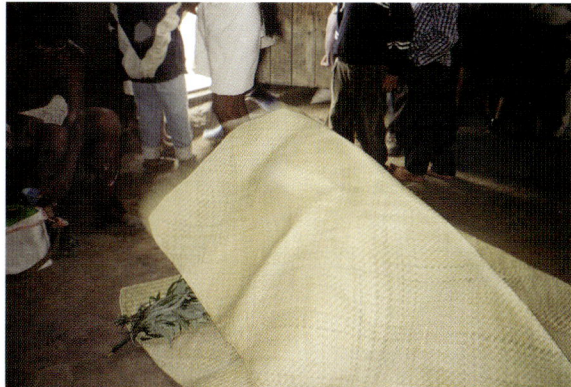

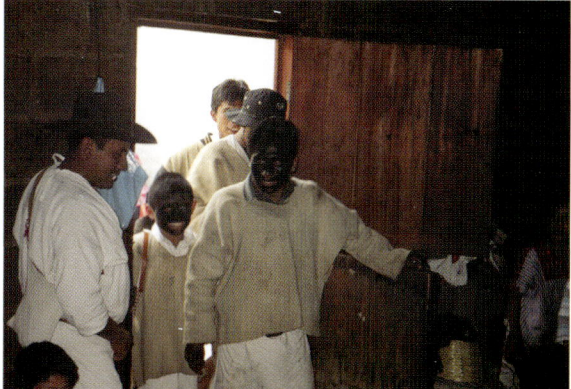

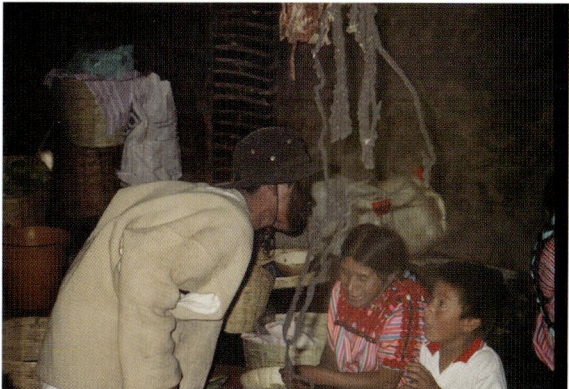

Above, The BoozeMeasurer; top right, hiding out, middle right, Blackmen break in, bottom right, Blackmen as dogs.

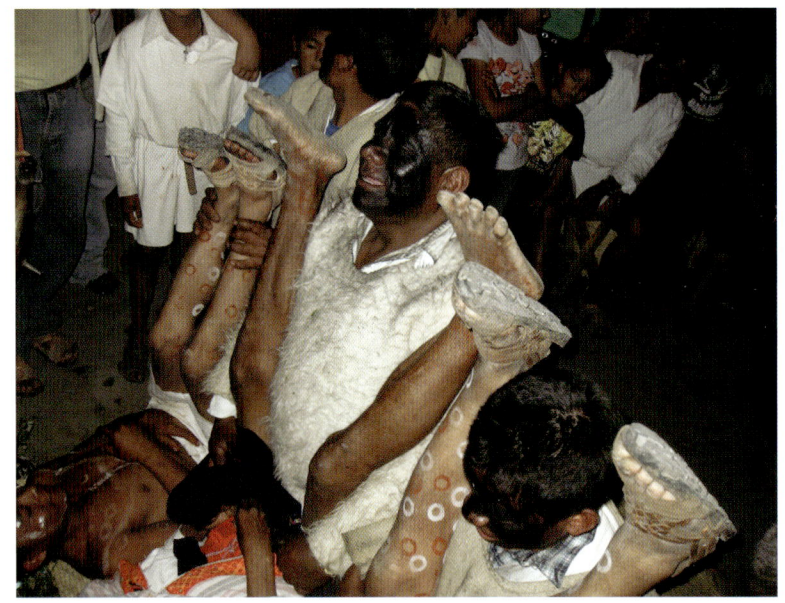

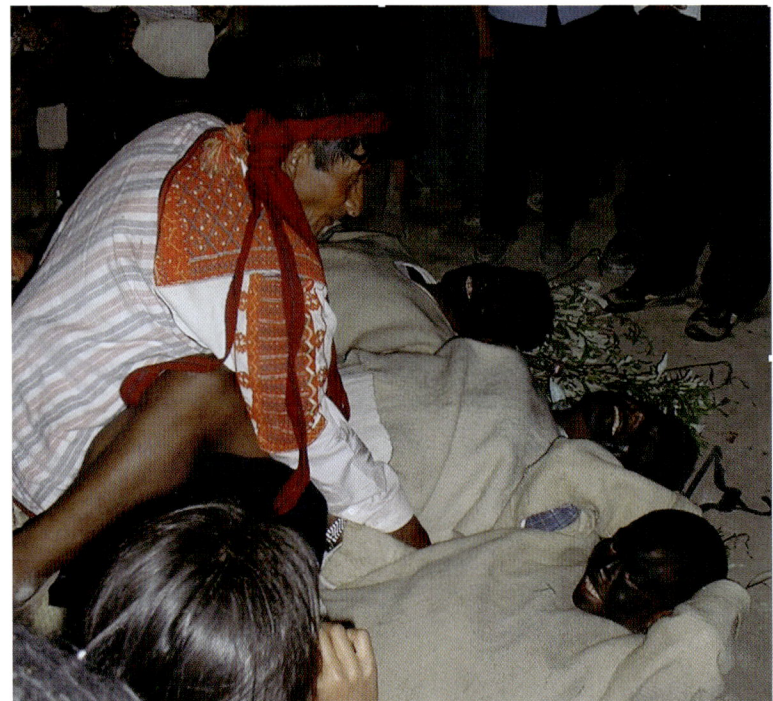

them. Women! Girls! If your husband isn't giving it to you right, if he hasn't made a baby with you yet, you had better come in here close and learn how it's done!"

Then the Blackmen get down on their knees and grab the Jungle Mother and the Crossbacks and pull up their legs and pretend to have sex with them. When they're done, they fall down and pass out, exhausted.

Jungle Mother and the Crossbacks get up. She calls for the advisor.

"Yes? What happened?" says the BoozeMaster.

"I'm going to have to do something about these men," the Mother says. "They came here meaning to pound me and I'm going to pay them back."

She and the Crossbacks lift the legs of the sleeping Blackmen and the Mother says, "Ladies, children, come watch if you don't know how this is done, take a look at this other way we'll show you. If you know how to give it then you also should learn how to take it too!"

Then she and the Crossbacks pretend to mount the Blackmen.

When they finish, the Mother calls out, "Mr. Passion? Mr. BoozeMeasurer?"

"What's up?"

"This didn't work!"

"Must be because you've got such a big one."

"But I didn't give him all of it. I only put in half!"

"Is that all? I thought it wouldn't fit because you'd given him the whole thing."

"It's true…once I got going I couldn't stop myself, so he did get it all… Well, never mind, we're going to have to bless them to wake them up. Could I have some water please?"

They pass Jungle Mother a bowl. Taking water in her mouth, she sprays it on the sleeping Blackmen, then tosses the rest off over her shoulder. (The people the water lands on laugh at that.) But the Blackmen don't stir.

The Mother says, "Well, that didn't work. Maybe we can wake them up with our branches," and she and the Crossbacks take the willow leaf bundles they used to cure the officials earlier and swipe them across the chests of the sleeping Blackmen. But the three Blackmen sleep on. (Well, then their leader wakes up enough to pull Jungle Mother's skirt out and look up underneath). She is hardly upset about this, treats it as a minor irritation, laughing.)

The Mother says, "Hm, even that doesn't seem to do it. Well, we will just have to leave them there. Passion, other officials, women officials, spectators, boys and girls, we're going now."

She and the Crossbacks exit the house on the run, singing as they go. They are off to hide in another Passion's house, get down under a new mat, and begin the little play all over with other Blackmen. (The Mother and the Crossbacks enact the mat drama four times in an afternoon—at the homes of two Passions leaving office and two entering.) Once they are gone, the Blackmen, those ferocious figures of darkness, arise and relax (one guy lights up an after-sex cigarette) and then make up a kind of soup called *wokol ich* (birth of chili?) and also called *kamaron*. (It contains dried shrimp, available in markets in the highlands.) The women pass them a small pail with onion greens in it. They heat it very briefly over a cooking fire, then go to the advisors, who add liquor. The Blackmen offer it around. I saw a man who had been lying back (sleeping? ill?) refuse, but it looked as though one of the women of the household was going to get a gourd bowl and drink some.

   The Blackmen are then paid in bottles of liquor. (The Mother and the Crossbacks received their payment in pox before the Blackmen showed up.)

   [Dialogue of the play from a recording I made in 2010, kindly translated to Spanish by Pedro Moshan and by me to English.]

The Jungle Mother during the creation of our world

In Victoria Bricker's *The Indian Christ, the Indian King* my old friend uses a variety of written sources from Chiapas and the Yucatán to connect historical events since the 16th century Spanish Invasion to elements in Maya fiestas in the 20th century. The associations she derives are illuminating and compelling, rich with long-stored Maya recollections of periods of resistance, violence, oppression. But the connections made necessarily contain elements of well-informed guess work. In *Renewing the Maya World: Expressive culture in a highland town* (2000), Garrett W. Cook pays homage to Victoria's achievement but his own insights about meaning in Maya fiestas in Guatemala come from more recent understandings of pre-Invasion cosmology in the work of archeologists, epigraphers, and interpreters of the *Popol Vuh* and other Maya texts. Thus, for example, in one town a wire is secured from the top of the village church to the ground and male actors dressed as the "original animals" in Maya creation stories descend from "Heaven" (the church) along it. Cook assumes the fiesta scenarios were created by members of the so-called "Quiche elite," the scholar storytellers who gave us the *Popol Vuh* soon after the Spanish Invasion. Cook thinks it not clear whether all of the passed-down symbolic actions are still understood either by performers or audience in the present. What matters most now, he says, is performing the rituals correctly.

Bricker understands Me'kabinal (Jungle Mother) as representing generations of lowland chiefs brought to the highlands along with recruited black soldiers to suppress indigenous rebellions like the one called "The War of the Virgin" in 1712. But Me'kabinal also makes a brief appearance in Chenalho's set of myths about *Ojoroxtotil* (most likely originally in Tsotsil *Ahau Riox Totil* or "Lord God Father.") He is a human-but also clearly god-like figure whose adventures are set in the period of Maya creation when the gods were still making up the world we know through trial and error.

One set of Ojoroxtotil stories appear in *Perils of the Soul* provided to ethnographer Calixta Guiteras-Holmes by Manuel Arias (Guiteras-Holmes p. 182 ff). Manuel's son Dr. Jacinto Arias Pérez gives more extensive versions of the tales in his *San Pedro Chenalho'*. The following account is translated and summarized from that book, pp. 30ff.

The world is a scary place during the early days of Creation. People can't go anywhere because there are tigers (jaguars?) ready to eat them, and fearsome black men with long hair. Assaults take place all the time. Ojoroxtotil tricks the tigers, slays most of them. Meeting a woman on the road, he finds a fertile spot and asks her to urinate there. Where she does it, chayote and squash grow up.

He encounters the Jungle Mother washing and bathing herself by a river. He changes himself into a dog and lifts the lady's petticoat with his teeth. She tries to frighten the dog away, but he won't let go of her. Ojoroxtotil goes and stays at Jungle Mother's house, bringing along his son. The Mother has daughters. A couple of days later the son disappears. The belly of the youngest of the sisters begins to swell rapidly. Angered, her father says, "Well, then, now since your son suddenly disappeared, we'll open up the girl's stomach." This worries the girl's older sisters. They tell Ojoroxtotil to take her because their father isn't fooling. Ojoroxtotil flees, carrying the little woman with him. Along the road he produces magic which plays with time, for example asking a man planting corn to tell the pursuers that's what he was doing when Ojoroxtotil came by, then making the corn immediately grow up and be ready to harvest.

Eventually, the girl's baby is born. The pursuers join forces against Ojoroxtotil because it turns out he is married to the Virgin Mary. The kings and the devils pester her because she's pretty. They want to be married to her themselves. They are about to kill Ojoroxtotil but he turns himself into stone and disappears.

Not only from the scene, but from the story as well. The narrative then takes up the son of the union of…is it Ojoroxtotil's son and the Jungle Mother's daughter…or Ojoroxtotil himself and the Jungle Mother? The new protagonist turns out to be some version of Jesus. The evil forces want to kill him. He says it doesn't matter, "Maybe I don't want to live…but I'm not going to die just here, I will die on the Holy Sceptre, on a cross.."

The Ojoroxtotil story covers the period when human life was fraught, its dangers mitigated only by the resourcefulness of the hero. And it turns out he is the spouse of the Virgin, and thus he (or is it his son?) is the father of Jesus and either way Jungle Mother is grandmother to Christ.

How much of the Ojoroxtotil legend is carried by people in Chenalho' today I do not know. But it's likely there's some connection in their minds between the tale and the transvestite character of today which adds meaning to Jungle Mother painting Jesus's sandals onto her feet. Ojoroxtotil's turning into a dog and grabbing the Mother's petticoat

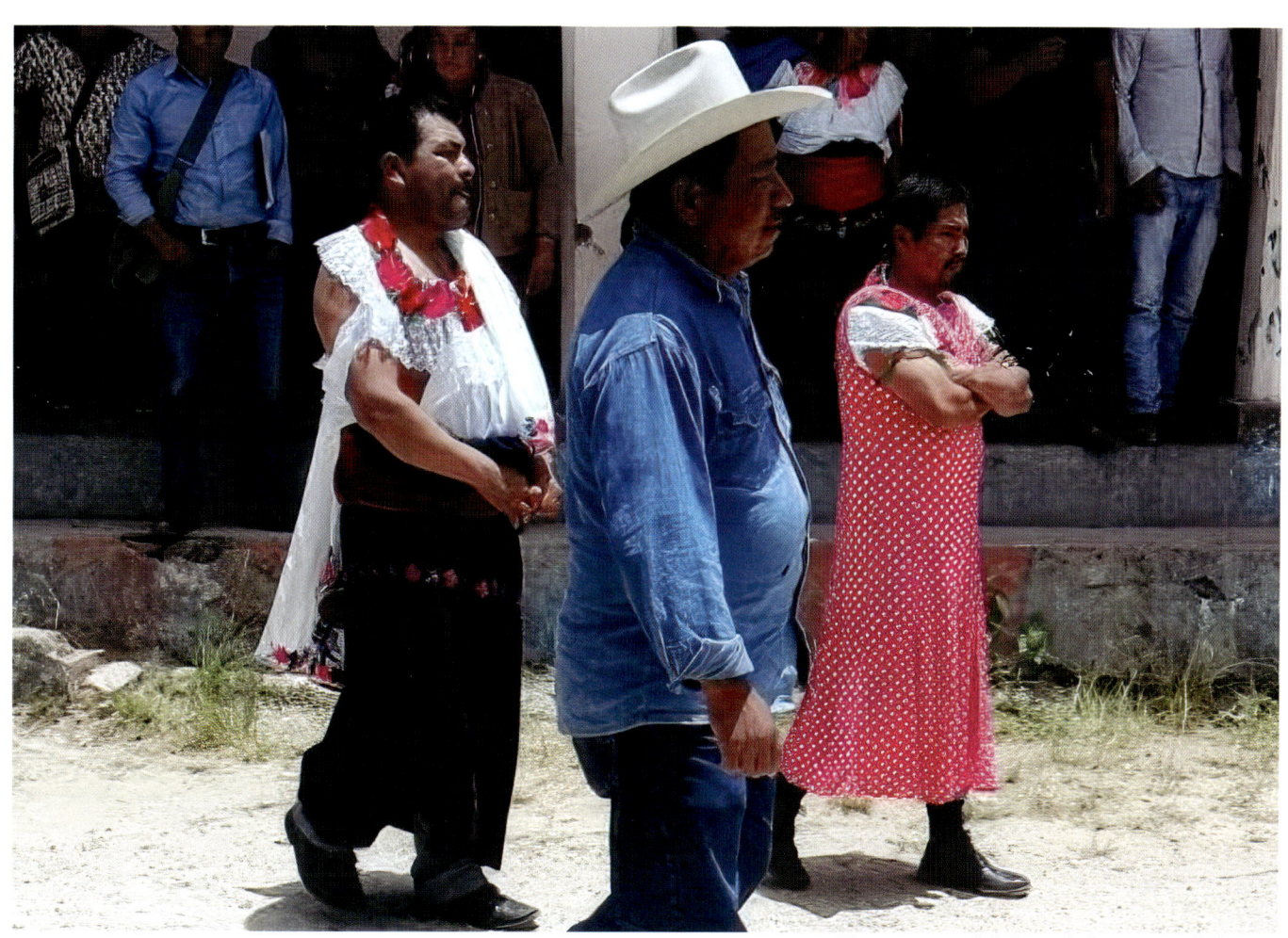

Two men paraded through the streets of Huistán

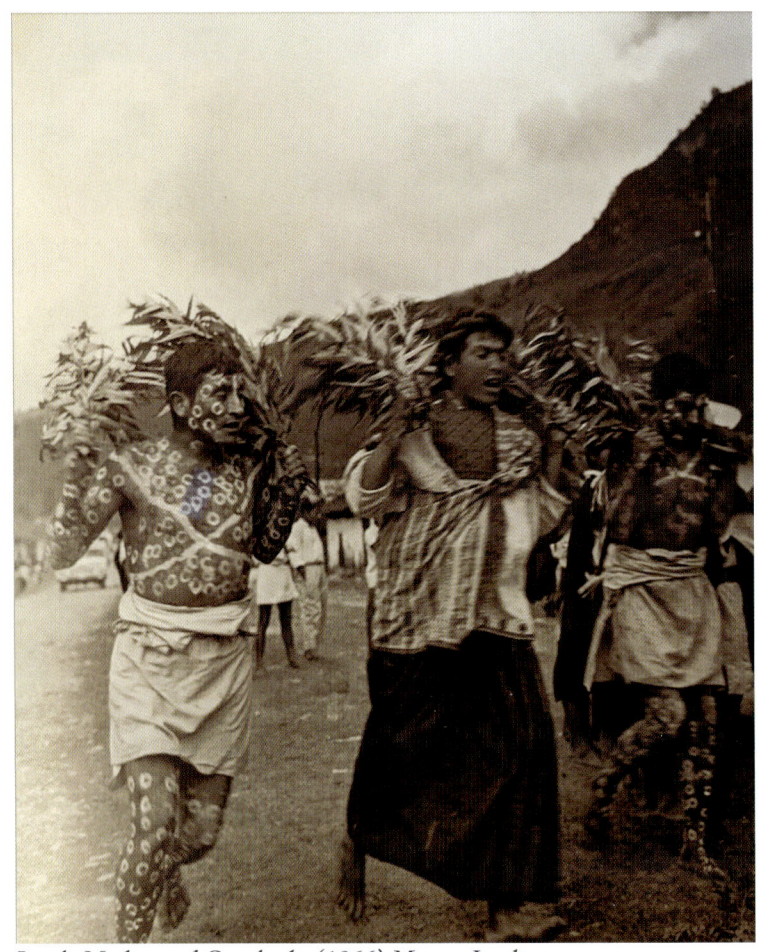

Jungle Mother and Crossbacks (1966) Marcey Jacobson

is directly reflected in the two Blackmen becoming dogs during the mat ceremony, and certainly in one Blackman grabbing hold of the Mother's skirt and looking up under it.

History has a mildly repetitive moment.

That first year at Nazarena Ámbar, Andrew, and I stayed through Tuesday. By then with drinking and sweating and running about to follow the events as they unfolded, we were fairly funky. Ámbar suggested we go down to the river to bathe. We crossed to the far side and walked along a narrow tree-shaded path looking for pools between the boulders in the water where we could immerse ourselves. When we found a couple of likely spots we started to undress. Across the way well above us was a woman hanging out wash on a line and looking down on us.

Ámbar called out to her. "Señora, we were going to bathe here."

"Well go on," the woman called back.

"We were going to take off our clothes, if you don't mind?"

"Why should I mind? Do you think I have all day to stand around here watching you?" Laughter all around.

And then she sent two of her little sons down in just their shorts to show us the best places to get ourselves well down into the cold, wonderful water.

Why finally?

The man who was Jungle Mother in my day had belonged to the Jtoyk'in for at least 44 years. Here he is on the left as a Crossback in Marcey Jacobson's photograph from 1966.

In 2010 he was 75 and sometimes his Crossbacks were played by his own grandsons. He wondered aloud to Ámbar and me about how much longer he could continue all the leaping and running around.

The general anthropologists' understanding of men in skirts in highland fiestas has been that they burlesque sexually inappropriate behavior by Maya women or by non-indigenous women who lord it over original people, ladinas who are demeaning, lewd, sacrilegious. (In Chamula the transvestite character *Nana Mama Cocarina* squats over the holy drums called the *bajbin* to render them ineffective through the well-known cooling power of a woman's exposed backside). But in the Festival of Games in Chenalho' the Guatemalan Woman is the only one of the big four crossdressers who comes close to fitting the old analysis.

The Jungle Mother's speeches in the Ceremony of the Mat may be bawdy, but her overall aspect is that of a force for good. (If she is included in the prediction that "Evil is coming," then I think we're safe.) I have not seen the Abductress's versions of the little play, but I imagine it is quite similar to the one with the Jungle Mother, the Crossbacks, and the Blackmen.

In the highlands men who play the parts of women in fiestas are under no stigma of being thought of as homosexuals. They are respected for their contributions to the fun. (Based on very limited data, I have the feeling that though men may sometimes have casual sex with other men, the idea of a person—man or woman—being a full-time homosexual still does not really exist in the Tsotsil municípios. When I asked the writer and indigenous scholar Xun Okotz about this, he offered the case of a vendor in the market in Tuxtla, the state capital, who was said to be a man one month and a woman the next, but that was as close as Xun could come.)

By contrast, in the Yucatán towns there are men who live and dress as women in daily life, some respected enough, in charge of the local cultural center or running hostels for boys from elsewhere attending a local school. Some of the men living as women in the peninsula are flamboyant in the style of drag queens in Mexico City and the U.S.

But the highland/lowland distinction about cross-dressing is not absolute. Forcing men to dress as women in public to shame them occurs, for example in the Tsotsil municipio of Huistán, where in the recent past two officials were caught in criminal activity and forced to parade through town, one in a *mestiza* dress and the other in traditional woman's clothing.

And in the Chiapas Tojolabal Maya communities close to the Guatemalan border there are men who live as women and are treated as ordinary citizens. Some of them however quit their home towns and follow traveling carnivals and circuses as cooks or whatnot and are sometimes called *muxe* after the well-known males in the Isthmus of Tehuantepec who live and work as women in their adult lives.

But why finally men in skirts in fiestas instead of actual women in those parts? "Actual" women have roles as well, carrying saints in processions, sometimes acting as majordomos themselves. In Chenalho' at the close of Tuesday there is a ceremonial exchange of liquor among the officials in the plaza attended not only by men but by wives and daughters as well, all dressed up in their best huipils and with their hair freshly washed and combed, some braided with ribbons.

I meet Chenalho'-born anthropologist, writer, and Maya scholar Jacinto Arias in San Cristóbal at a tiny coffee shop. When I ask Jacinto why the transvestite actors, he says he thinks it is because in the upside-down of fiestas like Tajimoltik our world in its entirety comes forth, history and legend stand side by side, and in the fun of the burlesque real females would do damage to their reputations as respectable "true women," so men have to put on skirts to portray the wild creatures which come from our history and our dreams.

I find Jacinto's answer entirely satisfactory.

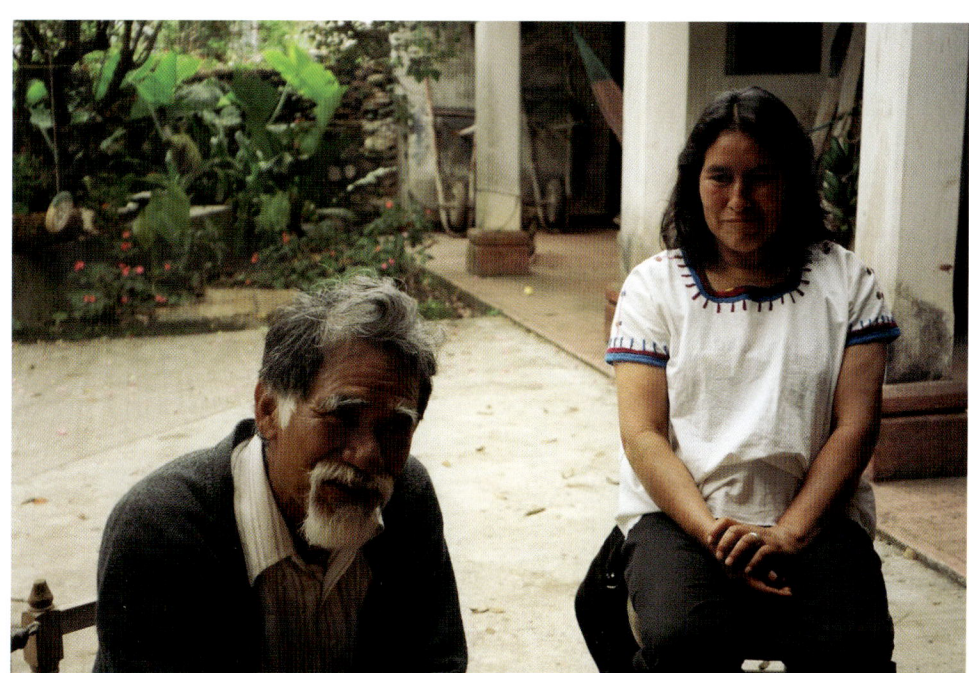

Jacinto Arias and his wife Marcela

Acknowledgements

Heartfelt thanks to Judith Aissen, Macduff Everton, and Ambar Past, all three ever generous. Also many thanks to Jacinto Arias, Victoria Reifler Bricker, Nicholas F. Bunnin, Allen J. Christenson, Randy Clark, Dra. Beatriz De Angotia, Christine Eber, Petra and Loxa Ernandes, Louanna Furbee, Mary Heeber, the late Robert Laughlin, Jennifer Mathews, Maruch Méndes Péres, Margarita Martínez Pérez, the late Xun Méndes Tsotsek and the late Walter F. "Chip" Morris, Pedro Moshan, the late June Nash, Joan and Barry Norris, the late Xun Okotz, Diane and Jan Rus, Victor Sagastume, the late George Sisson, Saideé Suárez. And special thanks to Leslie Marmon Silko for her wisdom about the sacred.

Bibliography

Anderson, Thor. (Director) *Sacred Games* (film) University of California Extension Media, 1988.

Arias, Jacinto. *San Pedro Chenalho': Algo de su historia, cuentos y costumbres.* Tuxtla Gutiérrez, Chiapas, Publicación Bilingue de la Dirección de Fortalecimiento y Fomento a las Culturas de la Subsecretaria de Asuntos Indigenas, 1985.

Beverton, Gary. *Maya for Travelers and Students: a guide to culture and language in Yucatan.* Austin, University of Texas Press, 1996.

Baskin, Arnold. (Director) *Appeals to Santiago* (film) University of California Extension Media, 1967 and 1974.

Bazetti, Michael (translator). *The Popol Vuh.* Minneapolis, Milkweed Editions, 2018.

Bricker, Victoria. *The Indian Christ, the Indian King.* Austin, University of Texas Press, 1981.

_____, *Ritual Humor in the Highlands of Chiapas.* Austin, University of Texas Press, 1973.

Christenson, Allen J. *The Burden of the Ancients: Maya Ceremonies of World Renewal from the Pre-Columbian Period to the Present.* Austin, University of Texas Press, 2016.

Cook, Garrett W. *Renewing the Maya World: Expressive culture in a highland town.* Austin, University of Texas Press, 2000.

De Landa, Fra Diego. *Relación de las cosas de Yucatán*, translated by William Gates. Dover Publications, 2012.

Eber, Christine. *Women and Alcohol in Highland Chiapas.* Austin, University of Texas Press, 1995.

Edmonson, Munro S. *The Book of Counsel: the Popol Vuh of the Quiche Maya of Guatemala.* Middle American Research Institute, Publication 35, Tulane University, New Orleans, 1971.

Ernantes Kusman, Petul. *Carnaval en Tenejapa, una comunidad Tzeltal de Chiapas.* Centro de investigaciones y estudios superiores en antropologia social: Archivo fotografico indigeno, Mexico, DF, 2005.

Guiteras-Holmes, Calixta. *Informe de San Pedro Chenalho'.* Manuscript on Middle American Cultural Anthropology, no. 14. The University of Chicago Library, 1946.

_____, *Perils of the Soul: the world view of a Tzotzil Indian*. New York, The Free Press of Glencoe, Inc., 1961.

Hrdy, Sarah Blaffer. *The Blackmen of Zinacantán*. Austin, University of Texas Press, 1972.

Lawrence, D.H. "Indians and Entertainment" in *Mornings in Mexico*, London, Martin Seckler, 1927, 97---118.

Morris, Walter F., and Jeffrey J. Foxx, *Living Maya*. New York, Harry N. Abrams, Inc., 1987.

Nash, June. *The Passion Play in Maya Indian Communities. Comparative studies in society and history*, 1968-04, Vol.10 318--327

Past, Ámbar, Ernandes, Petra, *Okotz, Xun, eds. Incantations: Songs, spells and images by Maya women*. San Cristóbal de Las Casas, Chiapas, Taller Leñateros, 2005.

Roscoe, Will, *The Zuni Man-woman*. Albuquerque, University of New Mexico Press, 1991.

Wilson, Carter, "Expression of Personal Relations through Drinking," in Siverts, Henning, ed. *Drinking Patterns in Highland Chiapas*. Bergen, Norway, Universitetsforlaget, 1973, 121---146.

_____, *Hidden in the Blood, a personal investigation of AIDS in the Yucatán*. New York, Columbia University Press, 1994.

_____, A review of Garrett W. Cook's Renewing the Maya World: Expressive culture in a highland town. *The American Ethnologist*, Fall, 2002.

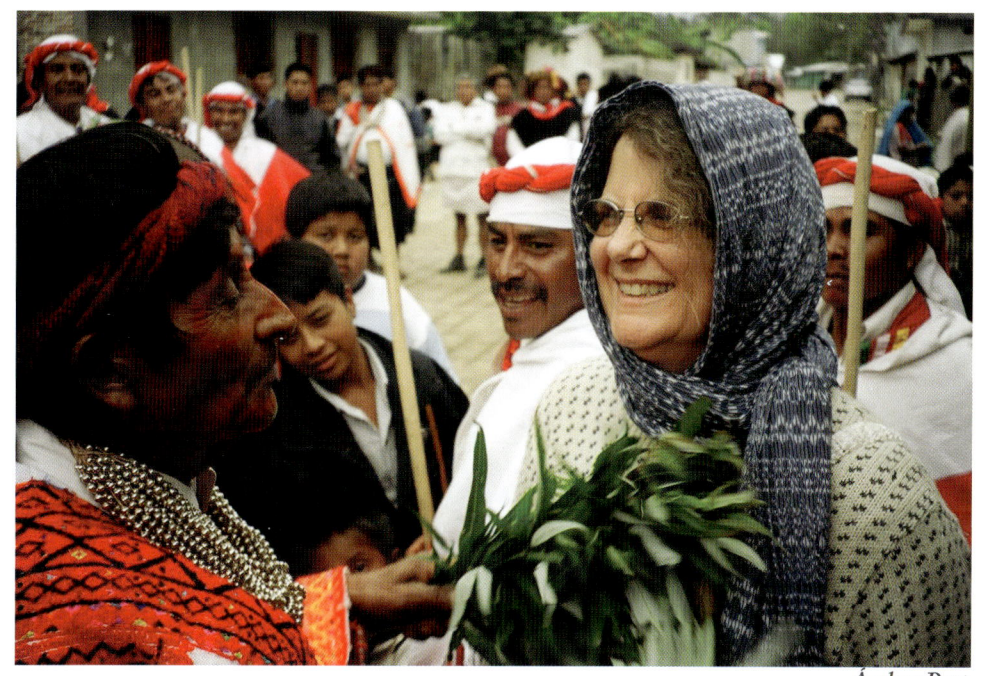

Ámbar Past